Thinking Critically: Animal Rights

Other titles in the *Thinking Critically* series include:

Thinking Critically: Animal Rights

Melissa Abramovitz

ReferencePoint
Press®

San Diego, CA

© 2018 ReferencePoint Press, Inc.
Printed in the United States

For more information, contact:
ReferencePoint Press, Inc.
PO Box 27779
San Diego, CA 92198
www.ReferencePointPress.com

Picture Credits:
Charts and graphs by Maury Aaseng

LIBRARY OF CONGRESS CATALOGING-IN-PUBLICATION DATA

Name: Abramovitz, Melissa, 1954- author.
Title: Thinking Critically: Animal Rights/by Melissa Abramovitz.
Other titles: Animal rights
Description: San Diego, CA: ReferencePoint Press, Inc., 2018. | Series: Thinking Critically | Includes
    bibliographical references and index.
Identifiers: LCCN 2016047506 (print) | LCCN 2017004546 (ebook) | ISBN 9781682822630
    (hardback) | ISBN 9781682822647 (eBook)
Subjects: LCSH: Animal rights--Juvenile literature. | Animal welfare--Juvenile literature.
Classification: LCC HV4708 .A237 2018 (print) | LCC HV4708 (ebook) | DDC 179/.3--dc23
LC record available at https://lccn.loc.gov/2016047506

Contents

Foreword

"Literacy is the most basic currency of the knowledge economy we're living in today." Barack Obama (at the time a senator from Illinois) spoke these words during a 2005 speech before the American Library Association. One question raised by this statement is: What does it mean to be a literate person in the twenty-first century?

E.D. Hirsch Jr., author of *Cultural Literacy: What Every American Needs to Know*, answers the question this way: "To be culturally literate is to possess the basic information needed to thrive in the modern world. The breadth of the information is great, extending over the major domains of human activity from sports to science."

But literacy in the twenty-first century goes beyond the accumulation of knowledge gained through study and experience and expanded over time. Now more than ever literacy requires the ability to sift through and evaluate vast amounts of information and, as the authors of the Common Core State Standards state, to "demonstrate the cogent reasoning and use of evidence that is essential to both private deliberation and responsible citizenship in a democratic republic."

The *Thinking Critically* series challenges students to become discerning readers, to think independently, and to engage and develop their skills as critical thinkers. Through a narrative-driven, pro/con format, the series introduces students to the complex issues that dominate public discourse—topics such as gun control and violence, social networking, and medical marijuana. All chapters revolve around a single, pointed question such as Can Stronger Gun Control Measures Prevent Mass Shootings?, or Does Social Networking Benefit Society?, or Should Medical Marijuana Be Legalized? This inquiry-based approach introduces student researchers to core issues and concerns on a given topic. Each chapter includes one part that argues the affirmative and one part that argues the negative—all written by a single author. With the single-author format the predominant arguments for and against an issue can be synthesized into clear, accessible discussions supported by details and evidence including relevant facts, direct quotes, current examples, and statistical illustrations. All volumes include focus questions to guide students as they read each pro/con discussion, a list of key facts, and an annotated list of related organizations and websites for conducting further research.

The authors of the Common Core State Standards have set out the particular qualities that a literate person in the twenty-first century must have. These include the ability to think independently, establish a base of knowledge across a wide range of subjects, engage in open-minded but discerning reading and listening, know how to use and evaluate evidence, and appreciate and understand diverse perspectives. The new *Thinking Critically* series supports these goals by providing a solid introduction to the study of pro/con issues.

The Animal Rights Debate

On August 17, 2016, animal rights advocates staged a protest at the Barnes & Noble bookstore in New York City where actress Amy Schumer was signing copies of her book, *The Girl with the Lower Back Tattoo*. The book was not the issue; rather, the fact that Schumer had previously worn a fur coat made by the Canada Goose company triggered the protest. "They torture and murder animals for their fur,"[1] one protester shouted.

In contrast to this peaceful protest, on July 22, 2016, radical animal rights activists cut locks, damaged fences, and freed a screech owl at a zoo in Athens, Georgia, to protest zoo confinement of wild animals. However, the activists were unaware that the zoo was caring for the owl because injuries prevented it from flying. "It was a pretty selfish act by uninformed people," said zoological coordinator Clint Murphy. "If they . . . want to free the animals, they are ignorant, because these animals cannot live on their own. They pretty much condemned that owl to a slow death."[2]

Welfarists Versus Abolitionists

These events reveal much about the contemporary animal rights movement and debate, which centers on whether animals deserve rights and freedom from human domination. There is often confusion over what is meant by the term *animal rights movement* because animal advocates fall into two main factions: welfarists and abolitionists. Welfarists, or protectionists, may or may not support human-like rights for animals, but they do advocate using education and anticruelty laws to reduce cruelty toward animals. In contrast, abolitionists, or liberationists, seek to end all human uses of animals and believe animals deserve human-like rights. The public often refers to individuals and organizations in both factions as animal rights activists.

Rutgers School of Law professor Gary L. Francione exemplifies the abolitionist position. "We have no moral justification for using nonhumans at all, irrespective of the purposes and however humanely we treat them," he writes in his book *The Animal Rights Debate: Abolition or Regulation?*, which he coauthored with welfarist Robert Garner. Liberationists like Francione believe the welfarist emphasis on gradual progress and legal reform is counterproductive. Welfarist achievements, as Francione puts it, "make the public feel more comfortable about animal exploitation" and require a "disturbing partnership between animal advocates and institutionalized exploiters."[3]

Evolutionary biologist Marc Bekoff, in contrast, supports the protectionist ideology. "Every action shines a light, whether it's motivated by a desire to change society or simply to fix one injustice in the life of one animal," he explains in his book *The Animal Manifesto*. "Every accomplishment, no matter how minor it seems, fuels our collective work on behalf of animals."[4] In line with this belief, Garner argues that liberationist ideologies are too "inflexible and dogmatic"[5] to be accepted by most people, who view animals as inferior to humans.

There is also much debate over which methods animal rights activists should use to achieve progress. The peaceful protesters at the Schumer book signing embraced lawful tactics that are often used by welfarists and by some liberationists to enhance public awareness of animal cruelty. In contrast, radical liberationists like those who vandalized the Athens zoo advocate using any means necessary—including violence—to achieve their goals.

Tactics and Results

The best-known radical abolitionist group, the Animal Liberation Front (ALF), is composed of independent underground cells that carry out illegal acts because they believe such acts—some of which are classified as terrorism—are effective. "Animal torture is a business," states a North

9

Strength of Animal Protection Laws Varies Widely

Illinois has the strongest animal protection laws in the nation while Kentucky has the weakest such laws, according to the 2015 Animal Legal Defense Fund (ALDF) report. The ALDF is involved in efforts to protect the rights and advance the interests of animals through the legal system. Its report, which has been produced annually for the last ten years, ranks animal protection laws in all fifty states. To arrive at these rankings the organization reviews fifteen different categories of laws, including those that address dogfighting and leaving an animal unattended in a vehicle. The 2015 report ranks states in three tiers: top, middle, and bottom tiers (with *top tier* referring to states with the strongest laws and *bottom tier* referring to states with the weakest laws).

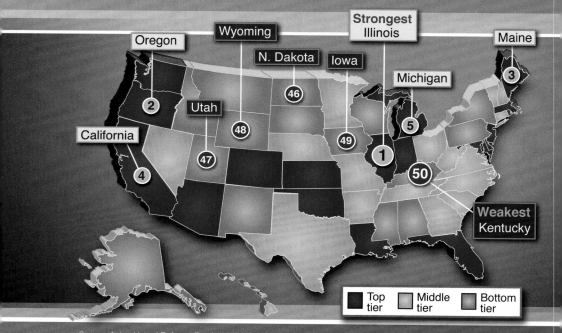

American Animal Liberation Press Office article. "We do not shut businesses with petitions and annual protests. We shut them down by destroying their profits and creating the personal detriments that make it too costly for them to continue."[6]

An attempted firebombing illustrates why ALF believes these tactics are effective. In June 2006 activists intended to firebomb the home of primate researcher Lynn Fairbanks of the University of California, Los Angeles, but they accidentally left a homemade bomb on the porch of Fairbanks's neighbor. It did not explode because of a faulty timer, but it did convince Fairbanks's associate, Dario Ringach, whose family had also been harassed by ALF, to tell ALF that he would no longer conduct primate research. "Dario Ringach is a poster boy for the concept that the use of force or the threat of force is an effective means to stop people who abuse animals,"[7] ALF press office director Jerry Vlasak told the *Los Angeles Times*.

Although radical abolitionists believe their actions are justified, law enforcement agencies and others who oppose their tactics call them terrorists. Psychologist Edwin A. Locke has particularly harsh words for such people. "The animal rights terrorists are like the Unabomber or the World Trade Center terrorists or Oklahoma City bombers," he wrote in an article for the *Los Angeles Daily News*. "They are not idealists seeking justice, but nihilists seeking destruction for the sake of destruction."[8]

Incremental Progress

Although studies indicate that the majority of people in the general public disapprove of ALF's tactics, protectionists enjoy more support from the public. This has helped them diminish animal suffering in industries like entertainment. For example, for several decades the Humane Society of the United States (HSUS) and other animal welfare groups aired videos documenting cruelty to circus animals, particularly elephants. The documented abuses included trainers poking and wounding elephants with hooked poles called bullhooks and chaining elephants in tiny pens for hours. The HSUS encouraged the public to boycott circuses and took legal action against the Ringling Bros. circus in particular.

In 2011 the owner of Ringling Bros., Feld Entertainment, paid the US Department of Agriculture (USDA) $270,000 to settle claims of violating the Animal Welfare Act (AWA). In 2016 and 2017, animal advocates achieved even bigger victories. In May 2016, the last elephant show occurred in Providence, Rhode Island, and Ringling Bros. moved its elephants to a conservation center in Florida. Then, in May 2017, the circus closed its doors completely.

Feld Entertainment said a variety of economic and social factors, including plummeting ticket sales after the elephant acts ended, led to Ringling Bros. closure. "We know now that one of the major reasons people came to Ringling Bros. was getting to see the elephants,"[9] stated chief operating officer Juliette Feld. But animal advocates and others believe the decision reflects changing public attitudes about animals in captivity. "The moment for elephants has passed," stated Matthew Wittman, curator of the Harvard Theater Collection and author of a book about circuses. "It's the same reason SeaWorld is retiring the orcas. There's a trend in American culture that watching exotic animals for entertainment is no longer a good thing."[10] Indeed, a 2016 survey of Providence residents found that 60 percent were happy the elephant acts were ending.

The History of Animal Rights

Most of the attitude and policy changes regarding animal welfare evolved over time as a result of the efforts of pro-animal activists. Although people have questioned the morality of using animals for food, labor, entertainment, and research throughout history, no real progress occurred until a clearly defined animal rights movement began in England during the eighteenth century.

Historians believe the philosophies introduced by British attorney Jeremy Bentham in 1781 jump-started the animal rights movement. Bentham was the first to formally argue that animals deserve legal protection rather than being "degraded into the class of *things*,"[11] as their legal status at the time mandated. Supporters began lobbying for laws to protect animals, and in 1824 they formed the first pro-animal organization, the Royal Society for the Prevention of Cruelty to Animals (RSPCA). The RSPCA's efforts resulted in anticruelty laws being passed despite staunch opposition. The group also opened the first animal shelters and veterinary hospitals during the 1840s and 1850s. During the 1860s the RSPCA launched antivivisection campaigns to stop medical experiments that involved live animals.

In 1866 social activist Henry Bergh started the American animal rights movement by founding the American Society for the Prevention of Cruelty to Animals in New York. Bergh and other activists began challenging everyday animal cruelty, such as horse-drawn carriage owners routinely whipping exhausted or lame horses. Their efforts led lawmakers to pass anticruelty laws despite resistance and ridicule from opponents who called them fanatics. Carriage drivers repeatedly threatened Bergh, and in a 1901 *Harper's Monthly Magazine* article, reporter Rupert Hughes joked that animal advocates like Bergh insisted that animals could vote and were entitled to "a few newspapers printed in their language."[12] The meatpacking, circus, hunting, fur-coat, and medical research industries also fought against the new laws. Indeed, these industries remain the most influential organized foes of animal advocates during the twenty-first century.

Over the years activists convinced Congress to strengthen animal welfare legislation with laws like the 1958 Humane Slaughter Act, the 1966 and 1970 Laboratory Animal Welfare Acts, and the 1972 Marine Mammal Protection Act. Gradually the attitudes of many individuals changed as well. Although the majority of Americans still consume animal products like meat and eggs, experts note that concern for animal welfare continues to grow during the twenty-first century. For example, a 2015 Gallup poll found that 32 percent of Americans believe humans and animals deserve equal rights (up from 25 percent in 2008), and a 2015 Harris poll found that 50 percent of Americans oppose using animals in research and 47 percent support it (compared to 43 percent who opposed and 52 percent who favored it in 2009). Many animal rights activists view these numbers as important milestones, particularly in light of humanitarian Mohandas Gandhi's famous proclamation: "The greatness of a nation and its moral progress can be judged by the way its animals are treated."[13]

Chapter One

Should Animals Have Rights Similar to Humans?

Animals Should Have Rights Similar to Humans

- Animals deserve rights and moral standing because they can feel and think.
- Animals deserve rights and moral standing because they are living creatures.
- Animals should not be considered human property because they are sentient, intelligent creatures with needs that transcend their usefulness to humans.

The Debate at a Glance

Animals Should Not Have Rights Similar to Humans

- Animals are inferior to humans and thus do not merit human-like rights.
- Animals cannot have rights because they cannot understand morality.
- Giving animals rights would lead to chaos because they could sue people for mistreating them; their current standing as human property is appropriate.

Animals Should Have Rights Similar to Humans

"While animals do not require human values such as the right to vote, they do need the same basic protective conditions rights assign for humans, namely the right to life, liberty, and the pursuit of happiness."

—Steven Best, an associate professor of philosophy and humanities at the University of Texas, El Paso

Steven Best, "Rethinking Revolution: Animal Liberation, Human Liberation, and the Future of the Left." www.drstevebest.org.

Consider these questions as you read:

1. Compare the utilitarian and deontological arguments about why animals deserve rights similar to those of humans. Which do you think is a stronger argument, and why?
2. Do you think that the capacity of certain animals to make moral judgments should qualify them for human-like rights? Why or why not?
3. What is your opinion about whether an animal's intelligence should determine the rights it is granted?

Editor's note: The discussion that follows presents common arguments made in support of this perspective, reinforced by facts, quotes, and examples taken from various sources.

Animals deserve similar rights as humans for several reasons, including their ability to feel pain and to think and their inherent value as living creatures. Animals also deserve rights because humans have harmed them throughout history by owning and abusing them, and it is time to end these injustices.

Animals Deserve Rights Because They Can Suffer

One argument that animals should have similar rights to humans comes from a way of thinking known as the utilitarian perspective. Utilitarians believe an act can be judged as right or wrong depending on its consequences. For example, a utilitarian would say that hitting a dog is wrong because the act causes the animal pain. Animal advocates who embrace a utilitarian philosophy believe that sentience—the ability to perceive, experience, feel, and particularly to feel pain—qualifies certain animals to be protected by human-like moral and legal rights. The first animal advocate to espouse this view was eighteenth-century British attorney Jeremy Bentham. "A full-grown horse or dog is beyond comparison a more rational, as well as a more conversible animal, than an infant of a day, or a week, or even a month, old," wrote Bentham to justify why animals deserve legal protection. "But . . . the question is not, Can they *reason*? Nor, Can they *talk*? But, Can they *suffer*?"[14]

Philosopher Peter Singer agrees. Considered the founder of the modern animal rights movement, Singer thinks animals' ability to suffer qualifies them for rights. "The capacity for suffering and enjoying things is a prerequisite for having interests," says Singer. "No matter what the nature of the being, the principle of equality requires that its suffering be counted equally."[15]

The Intrinsic Value of Animals

That animals should have similar rights to humans can also be argued from a deontological position. In contrast to the utilitarian position, supporters of deontological philosophies believe the inherent value of living creatures justifies granting them rights. The work of philosopher, musician, physician, and author Albert Schweitzer, who won the 1952 Nobel Peace Prize, heavily influenced the application of deontological ideas to animal rights. "Everything that lives has value simply as a living thing," said Schweitzer. "To the man who is truly ethical all life is sacred, including that which from the human point of view seems lower on the scale."[16]

The primary quality that makes living creatures intrinsically valuable is consciousness. Those who are conscious have an interest in furthering

Public Support for Giving Animals Rights Has Grown

Americans' support for giving animals the same rights as people has increased since 2003. Although the percentage of people saying animals should have *some* protections decreased between 2003 and 2015, the percentage of Americans who believe animals deserve the same rights as people rose from 25 percent in 2003 to 32 percent in 2015.

Support for Animals Having Same Rights as People

Which of these statements comes closest to your view about the treatment of animals?

- Animals deserve the exact same rights as people to be free from harm and exploitation.

- Animals deserve some protection from harm and exploitation, but it is still appropriate to use them for the benefit of humans.

- Animals don't need much protection from harm and exploitation since they are just animals.

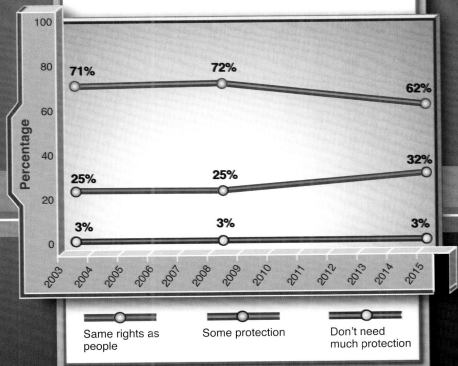

Source: Rebecca Riffkin, "In U.S., More Say Animals Should Have Same Rights as People." Gallup, May 18, 2015. www.gallup.com.

their own survival and leading the life for which their species was designed. Evolutionary biologist Marc Bekoff and other animal behaviorists have noted that animals struggle to escape impending death at slaughterhouses. This, coupled with their obvious dismay at the torture of their fellow creatures, reveals this interest in survival. Because animals have such interests, they need rights to protect them.

Philosopher Tom Regan, one of the best-known modern-day deontologists, refers to this quality as being "subjects-of-a-life," noting that it gives all living beings a "right to respectful treatment."[17] To Regan and others, the inherent value of human and animal lives is equal, so both deserve equal rights. Equal, however, does not mean identical. For instance, animals do not need the right to vote. But, like humans, they do need the right to be legally protected from, say, having people experiment on them.

Animals Share Human Qualities

Another reason animals deserve equivalent rights is that many of them display the same qualities—such as empathy and moral intelligence—as humans. For example, biologists often observe chimpanzees hugging and kissing fellow chimps who are grieving the loss of a family member; similarly, elephants are known to lift and carry injured comrades. Mammals have been observed acting morally toward other species as well. In one incident in Australia, a dog named Rex gently held a baby kangaroo in his mouth and brought it to a wildlife sanctuary after a car killed its mother. Animals "know right from wrong," writes Bekoff. "When beings are in need, animals will go out of their way to help them."[18]

Animals also possess intelligence, which also makes them a candidate for rights. Legal scholar and animal rights advocate Steven M. Wise notes that nonhuman primates, like gorillas and chimpanzees, have IQs between 70 and 95, which is very close to the average human IQ of 100. According to a cognitive and self-awareness intelligence scale that Wise has developed, humans rate 1.0, chimpanzees .98, gorillas .95, dolphins .90, African elephants .75, dogs .68, and honeybees .59. Wise proposes that animals with scores above .70 on the scale should be granted basic legal rights to liberty and bodily integrity, and those with scores below .50 should not. (Wise thinks those with scores between .51 and .70 should be granted rights that are proportional to their level of intelligence and self-awareness, though he acknowledges that such decisions are arbitrary, given humans' limited knowledge of animal intelligence.) Wise is the founder of the Nonhuman Rights Project, which has attempted to convince American courts to grant nonhuman primates legal personhood. "There is no rational reason why autonomous and self-determining nonhuman animals should not also possess equal and inalienable rights, recognition as a legal person, and rights to life, liberty, equality, security, and freedom from enslavement,"[19] he says.

> "There is no rational reason why autonomous and self-determining nonhuman animals should not also possess equal and inalienable rights, recognition as a legal person, and rights to life, liberty, equality, security, and freedom from enslavement."[19]
>
> —Legal scholar and animal rights advocate Steven M. Wise

Animals Deserve Independent Rights

Another reason why animals deserve similar rights as humans is that people have morally, physically, and emotionally harmed them by owning and abusing them throughout history, and it is time to end these injustices. Indeed, historical events have repeatedly proved that owning and subjugating living creatures for the benefit of some humans is morally wrong.

At one time, many Caucasians thought it was moral to own Africans as slaves because they perceived them as inferior. Similarly, a married woman was considered to be her husband's property, or chattel, with no legal rights, for the same reason. Slavery was outlawed in the United States in 1865, and some states began granting women independent rights in the 1840s. Gradually Americans realized that institutionalized racism, sexism, and other forms of discrimination were morally wrong, and this realization was codified in civil rights legislation that granted all humans equal rights. Similar laws have been passed in many places worldwide.

Just as it is wrong to deny basic rights to people who are considered different, it is also wrong to own nonhuman animals that some people perceive as inferior. This bias is known as speciesism—the belief that a creature's species determines its worth. Rutgers School of Law professor Gary L. Francione is one abolitionist who points out that protectionists who accept owning and using animals as long as the animals are treated nicely are equivalent to human rights advocates who once believed it was acceptable to own slaves so long as slaves were treated decently. African American author Alice Walker aptly frames the issue in the following way: "The animals of the world exist for their own reasons. They were not made for humans any more than black people were made for white, or women were created for men."[20]

> "From an ethical point of view, we all stand on an equal footing—whether we stand on two feet or four, or none at all."[21]
>
> —Philosopher Peter Singer

Liberationists have therefore proposed changing the term *animal owner* to *animal guardian*. Elliot Katz, founder of In Defense of Animals, was the first to promote this measure in 1999. Katz chose the word *guardian* because it means "protector." In fact, several cities and counties in the United States have legally enacted this change. In 2000, Boulder, Colorado, became the first to do so, legally changing the status of pet owners to pet guardians.

Although protectionists do not believe that ending human ownership of animals is necessary to grant them rights, they do agree that speciesism is morally wrong and must be abolished if animals are to receive the rights they are due. For instance, Singer argues that speciesism is a form of discrimination. "To discriminate against a being solely on account of their species is a form of prejudice, immoral and indefensible in the same way that discrimination on the basis of race is immoral and indefensible," he says. "From an ethical point of view, we all stand on an equal footing—whether we stand on two feet or four, or none at all."[21]

Animals Should Not Have Rights Similar to Humans

"Animals ought to be treated compassionately and kindly by people—because people can empathize with their pain but not because they have rights as human beings do. If they had such rights, they would, among other things, have to be held accountable for killing or maiming fellow animals in the wilds."

—Chapman University professor of business ethics Tibor R. Machan

Tibor R. Machan, "Animals Do Not Have Basic Rights," *New York Times*, April 5, 2012. www.nytimes.com.

Consider these questions as you read:

1. Some argue that animals should not be granted human-like rights because they lack the ability to understand morality and make moral decisions. In your opinion, what is the relationship between morality and rights? Must living creatures understand morality to have rights?

2. What is your opinion of Edwin A. Locke's contention that giving animals human rights will lead people to treat other people like animals? Do you think this would happen? Why or why not?

3. Some argue that ending human ownership of animals will lead to cases in which free animals with independent legal standing sue people for harming them. Do you think this is likely or unlikely to happen? Why or why not?

Editor's note: The discussion that follows presents common arguments made in support of this perspective, reinforced by facts, quotes, and examples taken from various sources.

Animals Do Not Need Rights

Animals do not need rights the way humans do. A better way to protect animals is to make sure people treat them humanely. Animals are not obligated to act morally, but humans are—they are therefore in the best position to protect animals from cruelty and suffering.

- Human beings have an awareness of moral ideas and understand the difference between right and wrong.

- Human beings accept that certain things are morally wrong and should not be done—regardless of whether the victim has any rights or not.

- Causing pain and suffering is morally wrong, whether the victim is a human animal or a nonhuman animal.

- This is not because it violates the rights of the victim, but because causing pain and suffering is inherently wrong.

- Causing pain and suffering therefore diminishes the moral standing of the human being that causes it.

- Therefore, human beings should not be cruel to animals.

Source: BBC, "Why Animals Don't Need 'Rights,'" 2014. www.bbc.co.uk.

Animals should not be given human-like rights because it is not sentience that qualifies a being for rights and moral standing. Rather, it is the ability to think rationally and make moral decisions. Humans have these qualities but animals do not, which makes humans superior to them and disqualifies animals for rights and membership in the moral community. Philosopher David Shoemaker defines a moral community as "an interplay between at least two agents, one who addresses a moral demand to the other . . . and the other, who ostensibly hears, understands, and either accepts or rejects the demand."[22] Thus, because animals—even intelligent ones like nonhuman primates—cannot make, understand, or respond to moral arguments, they cannot participate in the social relationships that underlie the need for rights.

Moral Understanding and Action

One reason why animals do not deserve rights is because they are incapable of translating moral understanding into action. "The purpose of morality is to provide a code of conduct that those in the moral community can use to guide their behavior," says philosophy professor Timothy Hsiao. "This presupposes that those in the moral community are *able to act* for moral reasons. The moral community is thus a community of rational and free beings."[23] Hsiao believes that since animals cannot be part of a moral community, they are not responsible for acting morally. When a lion eats a zebra, for instance, it is not acting immorally since it has no moral obligation to respect the rights of zebras. Thus, animals are not responsible for violating others' rights and also cannot accept the consequences of doing so. This lack of moral responsibility precludes them from qualifying for human-like rights.

> "To demonstrate that it possesses inviolable rights, a chimp or bonobo would need to do nothing less than stand up and, led by a love of justice and a sense of self-worth, insist that the world recognize and respect its dignity."[24]
>
> —Author and social commentator Damon Linker

Besides lacking the ability to have moral obligations and responsibilities, animals lack the sense of self and self-worth that would let them understand and describe why they deserve rights. Granting animals rights they cannot understand or defend would thus be futile because the purpose of human rights is to give rational beings legal and moral grounds to defend themselves from assaults on their person or property. As author Damon Linker argues, "To demonstrate that it possesses inviolable rights, a chimp or bonobo would need to do nothing less than stand up and, led by a love of justice and a sense of self-worth, insist that the world recognize and respect its dignity."[24]

The Religious Case Against Animal Rights

Human superiority to animals and entitlement to rights derives from one of humankind's oldest and most revered texts: the Bible. Indeed, several biblical passages discuss human superiority and dominion over animals, which helps justify the position that animals should not be granted human-like rights. Consider Genesis 1:26, which states, "And God said, Let us make man in our image, after our likeness: and let them have dominion over the fish of the sea and over the fowl of the air, and over the cattle, and over all the earth."[25]

Being made in God's image gives humans rights and responsibilities that animals lack. However, according to Brian Saint-Paul, editor of the Inside Catholic website, these rights come with "a moral obligation to care for animals, to protect animals, specifically because they do *not* have rights. They are completely and utterly at our mercy. So, as beings that have rights and have dignity and experience mercy from a merciful God, we have the absolute moral obligation to show mercy in kind."[26]

Disturbing Consequences

Not only should animals *not* be granted rights, but humans will suffer legal, moral, and everyday harm if animals are granted them. For example, Edwin A. Locke, who publicly debates animal rights activists on college campuses, believes that if animals are granted rights, the moral and practical differences between people and animals will be obscured. People will stop placing human interests above those of animals, which could even result in people treating other people like animals. "The animal 'rights' movement is not about the humane treatment of animals," he warns. "Its goal is the animalistic treatment of human beings."[27] Saint-Paul reaches a similar conclusion from a theological perspective, noting that if humans reject their unique status as superior creatures made in the image of God and "start treating animals like humans, it becomes that much easier to treat humans like animals."[28]

Furthermore, if animals are given rights similar to those of humans, people who are responsible for caring for them, and the animals that these people protect, could all face disastrous consequences. These consequences would be especially severe if animal liberationists achieve their goal of freeing animals from human ownership and granting them independent rights.

Both federal and state laws, such as the AWA and California's penal code 597, require that people who own animals must care for and treat them humanely. Offenders may be imprisoned and/or fined. The National Animal Interest Alliance (NAIA) notes that pet ownership is especially beneficial to animals: "US law is based on ownership of property, including animals. Property rights protect owners and their pets from unwarranted seizure by authorities and allow owners to make decisions about pet care, training, breeding, housing, and other matters."[29]

If animal ownership is terminated and animals are granted rights as independent organisms, the people who care for them—including the estimated 79.9 million American families who owned pets in 2016—would become their legal guardians. Existing legal standards consider guardians to be temporary caretakers who are responsible—together with the courts—for people such as children who cannot make their own decisions. But turning animal owners into guardians would require these temporary caretakers to seek a court's authority to provide certain types of care. This would create confusion about who is responsible for this care and could have dire consequences, including having no one legally responsible for feeding and protecting the animal. "Guardians care for the property of someone else. So, who will own pets if everyone is a guardian? The STATE?,"[30] the NAIA asks.

> "Guardians care for the property of someone else. So, who will own pets if everyone is a guardian? The STATE?"[30]
>
> —The National Animal Interest Alliance, an organization that protects both human and animal interests

Questions about responsibility under these circumstances have led some legal experts, like veterinarian and attorney Gerald L. Eichinger, to warn that anyone who believed an animal guardian was not properly caring for an animal could sue the guardian on the animal's behalf. Veterinarians could face similar lawsuits; in fact, Eichinger and others have warned that fears of such litigation would require many veterinarians to buy expensive malpractice insurance. In turn, these costs would be passed along to patients, and the cost of veterinary care would skyrocket. As long as animals are classified as human property, any lawsuits consider the owner to be the party that is wronged, and it is very difficult for an owner to collect damages. Veterinarians' malpractice insurance is thus fairly inexpensive, so long as animals remain human property.

Lawsuits initiated by People for the Ethical Treatment of Animals (PETA) have already foreshadowed the consequences of granting animals human-like rights. In 2012 the organization sued SeaWorld San Diego on behalf of five orcas whose rights they claimed were being violated. In 2015 it sued professional photographer David Slater on behalf of a macaque monkey named Naruto, who they claimed should own the copyright (and monetary proceeds) to selfies Naruto took after Slater left his camera unattended on a trip to Indonesia. Although both lawsuits were unsuccessful, they indicate the confusing—and expensive—consequences of granting animals certain kinds of rights.

Chapter Two

Is It Moral to Eat Animals?

It Is Moral to Eat Animals

- Animals have no moral standing, so it is moral to eat them.
- Eating meat is an integral part of human culture and the natural food chain.
- Animals exist for humans to use, so it is moral to eat them.
- Laws protect animals raised for food from being abused.

The Debate at a Glance

It Is Not Moral to Eat Animals

- Raising and killing animals for food causes these creatures great physical and emotional suffering.
- Laws designed to protect animals raised for food from abuse are ineffective and underenforced.
- Even so-called humane methods of raising and killing animals involve substantial abuse and suffering.
- Modern society and products make meat eating no longer necessary; people can get all the nutrition they need from plant-based foods and meat substitutes.

It Is Moral to Eat Animals

"Larger brains benefited from consuming high-quality proteins in meat-containing diets, and, in turn, hunting and killing of large animals, butchering of carcasses and sharing of meat have inevitably contributed to the evolution of human intelligence in general and to the development of language and of capabilities for planning, cooperation and socializing in particular."

—University of Manitoba environmental studies professor Vaclav Smil

Vaclav Smil, *Should We Eat Meat?* Oxford, UK: Wiley-Blackwell, 2013, p. 178.

Consider these questions as you read:

1. Do you think that biblical references to human dominion over and superiority to animals make it moral for people to eat them? Why or why not?
2. What is your opinion of the argument that eating meat is moral because it has been part of human culture throughout history?
3. Do you agree with the argument that the existence of the food chain makes it moral for humans to eat animals? Explain your answer.

Editor's note: The discussion that follows presents common arguments made in support of this perspective, reinforced by facts, quotes, and examples taken from various sources.

There are many reasons why it is moral to eat animals. Among them is the fact that animals have no moral standing and often exist primarily for human use. Moreover, eating meat is an integral part of human culture, and laws protect animals used for food from being abused. For these reasons and more, people can feel good about their choice to eat meat and consume other animal products.

A Long-Justified Morality

Biblical passages about God giving humans dominion over other creatures provide the earliest moral justifications for eating animals. For thousands of years, major world religions like Christianity and Judaism have used these passages as a guide for how to use animal products. "Part of the right God gives us is to use animals when necessary," explains Christian theologian Brian Saint-Paul. "Not to exploit them, but to use them for clothing . . . and most often for food."[31] He emphasizes that with this right comes the obligation to support humane methods of keeping and slaughtering animals. Judaism embraces similar justifications for and responsibilities associated with eating animals. In fact, traditional Jewish laws that govern kosher food—which prohibits Jews from eating certain animals like pigs or from mixing milk and meat—emphasize that food animals must be humanely slaughtered by a specially trained person in a way that minimizes the animal's pain and respects the sacrifice it is making to feed the person.

> "Part of the right God gives us is to use animals when necessary. Not to exploit them, but to use them for clothing . . . and most often for food."[31]
>
> —Christian theologian Brian Saint-Paul

The inability of animals to understand or act on moral rights and responsibilities also makes it moral to eat them. Just as animals do not act immorally when they eat other animals, people do not act immorally when they eat animals. As philosophy professor Timothy Hsiao puts it, "Since animals lack moral status, it is not wrong to eat meat." Hsiao also points out that even though consuming meat may involve animal suffering, humans are not guilty of *morally* harming them. "Although animals experience pain as it is physically bad, their experience is not in itself *morally* bad," he argues. "They are harmed in feeling pain, but this harm is not of a moral kind."[32]

Eating meat has always been culturally acceptable. People enjoy eating meat, and meat and other animal-based foods are important for optimal health. All of these reasons also make it moral to consume animals. Food journalist Michael Ruhlman points out that the pleasure he derives

Americans Think Meat Eating Is Moral

Data from the USDA and the Dutch financial firm Rabobank show that meat eating is either on the rise or has held steady since 2012. Americans are also likely to continue or increase their consumption of chicken, pork, and beef through at least 2018. This indicates that Americans think it is moral to eat animals and are unlikely to change their minds in the near future.

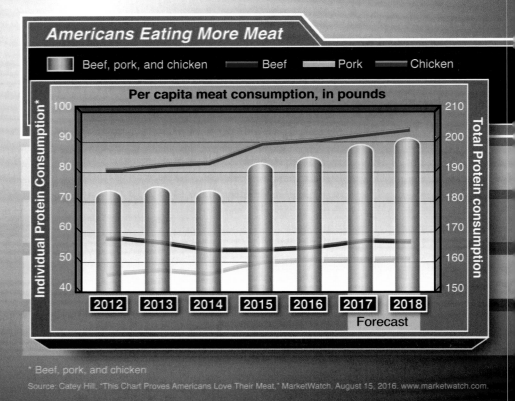

Americans Eating More Meat

Beef, pork, and chicken   Beef   Pork   Chicken

Per capita meat consumption, in pounds

Individual Protein Consumption*

Total Protein consumption

2012 2013 2014 2015 2016 2017 2018

Forecast

* Beef, pork, and chicken

Source: Catey Hill, "This Chart Proves Americans Love Their Meat," MarketWatch, August 15, 2016. www.marketwatch.com.

from eating meat is good for him personally and socially, noting that many social events center around traditions like grilling meat on a barbeque. This social cohesiveness, he believes, is a morally positive thing for humans. The health benefits of eating meat further underscore its morality, as it is morally right to strengthen one's body and mind. In fact, Ruhlman calls a vegan diet "a superlative weight-loss strategy"[33] because he and many others believe it does not provide enough calories or nutrients.

Research by evolutionary biologists and anthropologists supports the notion that eating meat is a natural, healthy, and culturally important practice. In 1999 anthropologist Katharine Milton published a study that confirmed her hypothesis that eating meat "played an absolutely essential role in human evolution."[34] Other scientific findings support Milton's evidence that when human ancestors incorporated meat into their diet, doing so provided the energy, calories, and nutrients required to grow the brain and body into those that characterize modern humans. It also facilitated social connections, as human ancestors gathered around a fire to cook the animals they had hunted. Eating meat thus became a healthy and integral part of human culture and society.

The fact that humans share classic predatory features with other meat-eating or omnivorous predators further supports the naturalness of eating meat. These features include eyes on the front of the face and teeth that are suited for eating meat. "By nature, humans are meat eaters, and our bodies are designed for it," says sports nutrition coach Kadya Araki. "We have incisors for tearing meat and molars for grinding it. If we were meant to subsist on vegetables alone our digestive system would be similar to that of the cow, with four stomachs and the ability to ferment cellulose in order to break down plant material."[35]

In addition, eating meat is consistent with the laws of nature that feature a food chain in which animals eat other species to survive. One well-known person who used the food chain argument to justify the morality of eating animals was politician, statesman, scientist, and inventor Benjamin Franklin. In his autobiography Franklin wrote that he temporarily stopped eating animals because he objected to their slaughter. But one day he and some friends were preparing a fish fry feast, and Franklin was tempted to try the delicious-smelling cod. While preparing the fish, he saw smaller fish taken out of the stomachs of larger fish. "If you eat one another, I don't see why we mayn't eat you,"[36] he reasoned before indulging in the first of many more animal-based meals.

Food Animals Have a Purpose

Meat eating is also moral when you consider that providing food for humans is the only reason many animals exist. "A great number of animals owe their lives to our intention to eat them," explains British philosopher

Roger Scruton. "Their lives are (or can easily be made to be) comfortable and satisfying in the way that few lives led in the wild could possibly be. If we value animal life and animal comfort, therefore, we should endorse our carnivorous habits, provided it really is life, and not living death, on which those habits feed." Scruton believes that as long as people think and act like what he calls "virtuous carnivores," who are concerned about how food animals are treated (as opposed to being "vicious carnivores"[37]) meat eating is moral.

Indeed, increasing numbers of people insist on buying humanely raised and slaughtered animals, and this elevates the morality of eating animals that are born and raised for this purpose. "I only eat meat when I know how it was raised. . . . I know exactly where to get products made with the sustainable and ethical practices I'm looking for," states Catherine Gerson, who works for the World Society for the Protection of Animals. "At the end of the day I am eating the animals that I 'protect' and I try to make a better life for."[38]

> "A great number of animals owe their lives to our intention to eat them. And their lives are (or can easily be made to be) comfortable and satisfying in the way that few lives led in the wild could possibly be."[37]
>
> —British philosopher Roger Scruton

Many consumers, businesses, and governments also support campaigns to eliminate the egregious abuses of food animals. For instance, more than twelve countries and several US states have banned foie gras (a fatty-liver delicacy) because of the cruelty involved in producing it. "Foie gras producers shove pipes down ducks' throats to force feed them far more than they would ever eat," says the HSUS. "Force feeding can cause bruises, lacerations, and sores. The duck's liver may grow to ten times the normal size."[39] By refusing to support this type of cruelty, meat eaters do much to enhance the morality of their dietary habits.

Laws Protect Animals

Opponents of eating meat often argue that even humane slaughter methods still involve animal cruelty. However, with a combination of federal and state laws that forbid cruelty to farm animals, these animals do not suffer unnecessarily or excessively. In particular, newer laws like California's Prevention of Farm Animal Cruelty Act, which voters passed in 2008 and which became active in 2015, prohibits confining farm animals to cages in which they cannot stand, lie down, turn around, or spread their limbs or wings.

In addition, government and private inspectors monitor compliance with anticruelty laws. Inspectors with the USDA Food Safety and Inspection Service, for instance, enforce standards for the housing, care, transport, and slaughter of food animals (except for poultry) at USDA-inspected facilities. The US secretary of agriculture is required to track and report any violations to Congress annually, and the USDA can impose fines and other penalties on offenders. Thus, laws support the morality of eating animals by protecting these animals.

It Is Not Moral to Eat Animals

"The amount of cruelty, pain, suffering, and death that takes place in factory farms far surpasses the total amount of cruelty, pain, suffering, and death in all other venues [industries] combined."

—University of Colorado, Boulder, ecology and evolutionary biology professor emeritus Marc Bekoff

Marc Bekoff, *The Animal Manifesto*. Novato, CA: New World Library, 2010, p. 115.

Consider these questions as you read:

1. Do you think the fact that the meat industry contributes to global warming makes it immoral to consume animals and animal products? Why or why not?
2. How do reports about the way food animals are treated affect your perception of the morality of eating meat?
3. Does the fact that people can get all the nutrition they need from a plant-based diet and meat substitutes influence your opinion of whether it is moral to eat meat? Why or why not?

Editor's note: The discussion that follows presents arguments made in support of this perspective, reinforced by facts, quotes, and examples from various sources.

When one really thinks about what is involved in consuming animals, he or she can only conclude that it is an immoral thing to do. Raising and killing animals for food subjects them to incalculable suffering, and laws designed to protect these animals are ineffective and underenforced. In addition, modern products make meat eating unnecessary. For these reasons and more, society should move beyond meat.

Incalculable Suffering

Animals suffer greatly, both emotionally and physically, throughout the process of being raised, transported, and slaughtered for food. This is supported by studies that show that cows and other animals raised for food suffer emotionally while watching their fellow creatures being hung by their rear legs at slaughterhouses as they wait in line to have their throats slashed. Cows witnessing these horrors often cry out; if they too were not slaughtered momentarily, they might cry and grieve for much longer, according to evolutionary biologist Marc Bekoff and other animal behaviorists who have witnessed dairy cows grieving after their babies were taken away to be slaughtered.

Food animals also experience emotional and physical agony when their deaths are prolonged during the slaughter process. This includes being stunned with electricity or hit on the head, then having their throats cut by a knife. For chickens, it involves being thrown into scalding water to remove their feathers. "Sometimes the blade that's intended to kill them misses their necks and they're plunged into the scalding water and drowned alive,"[40] says HSUS public policy coordinator Alicia Prygoski.

Suffering and associated stress also reduce the life spans of animals that provide food products like milk or eggs. For instance, according to the HSUS, most egg-laying hens live in cramped battery cages that average 67 square inches (432 sq. cm)—the size of a laptop computer. These spaces are so small that they are unable to move around and build nests, and they experience stress and pain from frequent broken bones. These conditions reduce their natural life span from about thirteen years to less than two.

In all, the food industry is responsible for more animal cruelty, suffering, and death than any other animal use. According to the USDA, each year about 9 billion land animals, including cows, pigs, chickens, turkeys, and sheep, are killed in the United States alone, which amounts to hundreds of thousands of deaths per minute.

Laws That Lack Teeth

Another reason why consuming animals is wrong is that anticruelty laws that are supposed to make the process of raising and slaughtering animals for food more humane are, in reality, quite weak and rarely enforced. "Investigations and industry whistle-blowers have revealed abuses on farms and in slaughterhouses so horrific, most people cannot even bear to witness them," notes the Animal Legal Defense Fund. "Farmed animals receive only minimal protections by our legal system."[41] In addition, although the USDA is authorized to inspect the 148 million cows, pigs, and sheep slaughtered each year, it only has about 150 inspectors to do so. This means that much abuse remains unseen and unpunished. These shortcomings make it immoral for people to support a system that routinely allows animal torture and exploitation. The meat industry and government will not be motivated to correct these abuses until the public stops buying meat.

> "Investigations and industry whistle-blowers have revealed abuses on farms and in slaughterhouses so horrific, most people cannot even bear to witness them."[41]
>
> —The Animal Legal Defense Fund

In addition, the AWA and many state anticruelty laws do not even apply to farm animals. Those that do apply fail to prohibit immoral standard industry practices, such as removing animals' testicles, tails, beaks, or horns without anesthesia. The Humane Methods of Livestock Slaughter Act's effectiveness is also limited because it excludes birds, which make up more than 90 percent of food animals. Numerous complaints about bird abuse led the USDA to adopt the Poultry Products Inspection Act in 2005, but the organization rarely enforces this law. In January 2015, for example, undercover investigators for the HSUS took videos of workers at a Minnesota slaughterhouse throwing sick chickens against walls, but the USDA did nothing. "USDA tends not to require animal agriculture to do anything it does not want to do,"[42] explains Dena Jones of the Animal Welfare Institute.

Another weak federal law is the Twenty-Eight-Hour Law, which requires vehicles that transport animals to slaughterhouses to stop every twenty-eight hours to give animals food, water, rest, and exercise. However, it is filled with loopholes, and there is no record of it ever being enforced since its inception in 1873. It also waives the twenty-eight-hour limit in the event of "accidental or unavoidable causes that could not have been avoided,"[43] such as a storm. Even if the law were enforced, twenty-eight hours is still a long time for animals to stand in a crowded truck or rail car with no food, water, or room to lie down.

Consuming Animals Harms the Planet

Raising and killing food animals also does significant damage to the environment, another reason why consuming these creatures is immoral. According to the Food and Agriculture Organization of the United Nations, livestock are responsible for 14.5 percent of the greenhouse gas emissions worldwide. Greenhouse gases trap heat and cause global warming, which in turn is already causing habitat destruction, rising sea levels and flooding, extreme weather, increases in insect-borne diseases, and other threats. Cattle produce 65 percent of all livestock-related emissions, which come from producing, processing, and transporting animals and animal feed and from enteric fermentation (cow farts) and the decomposition of their manure. A 2013 study by livestock researchers in Kenya, Australia, and Austria found that feeding and raising livestock also uses one-third of the world's freshwater supplies.

On the other hand, studies have found that cultivating and harvesting plant foods can reduce greenhouse gas production by up to 53 percent, compared to emissions produced from raising food animals. People who adopt a vegetarian or vegan diet thus help repair some of the environmental damage humans have wreaked. This is a moral thing to do because, as organizations like the Union of Concerned Scientists have warned, the planet will become uninhabitable if people fail to prevent global warming.

Humans No Longer Need to Eat Meat

There was a point in time at which humans required meat for nutrition—few other protein sources were available. However, in modern times, there are plenty of nonmeat choices (tofu, tempeh, mock meat products, protein powders, vitamins, and more) that provide complete nutrition. Thus, eating meat is no longer essential from a nutritional perspective.

Concern for Animals Is One Reason for Veganism's Rise

The number of vegans among young people in the United Kingdom has skyrocketed since 2006—and one of the reasons given for this change is concern about the morality of eating animals. A 2016 survey by the British newspaper the *Guardian* revealed a massive 350 percent increase in the number of vegans in the United Kingdom since 2006. Survey participants gave various reasons for why they decided to adopt a vegan lifestyle. Among the reasons given was concern about the treatment of animals and disgust with the idea of killing them for food.

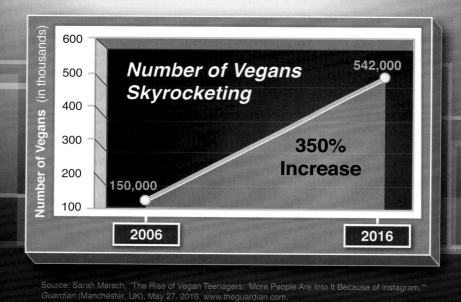

Source: Sarah Marsch, "The Rise of Vegan Teenagers: 'More People Are Into It Because of Instagram,'" *Guardian* (Manchester, UK), May 27, 2016. www.theguardian.com.

Eating less or no meat is also moral because it has been shown to reduce the risk of heart disease and some cancers. "A well-planned vegetarian diet can give you good nutrition. It often helps you have better health"[44] by reducing fat intake and obesity, according to the National Institutes of Health. A 2014 study by doctors at Loma Linda University concluded that vegetarian diets in which people consume no meat, but do eat eggs and milk products, help people live longer. The same was found true of vegan diets—in some cases, vegan diets conferred even greater protection against serious diseases. For example, vegetarians have a 55 percent lower risk of hypertension (high blood pressure) than nonvegetarians, and vegans have a 75 percent reduced risk compared to nonvegans. Overall, vegetarians and vegans have a 50 percent reduced risk of developing colon cancer, a 26 to 68 percent lower risk of dying from heart disease, and a 48 percent lower risk of dying from breast cancer. Caring for one's health is certainly moral, as is reducing the enormous amount that people and governments spend treating serious diseases each year.

> "A well-planned vegetarian diet can give you good nutrition. It often helps you have better health."[44]
>
> —The National Institutes of Health

The First Step

Perhaps most telling is that when people take the first step toward stopping animal consumption, they become more willing to commit to total ethical veganism, which involves not supporting any activity in which humans abuse animals, including wearing clothing that contains leather or fur. This is because they realize that exploiting animals—for any purpose—is morally unacceptable. As law professor Gary L. Francione says, animal consumption "is the primary practice that in effect legitimizes all other forms of exploitation."[45] Francione finds that when people stop eating meat, they are more likely to conclude that animals are living creatures that deserve dignity and compassion, which makes their subjugation and abuse immoral.

Chapter Three

Should Animals Be Used for Entertainment?

Animals Should Be Used for Entertainment

- Being entertained by animals is an integral part of human culture.
- There are many laws and regulations that ensure when animals are used for entertainment they are respected and treated well.
- Venues like zoos are educational resources and have positive ecological effects.

The Debate at a Glance

Animals Should Not Be Used for Entertainment

- Using animals for entertainment exploits these creatures for economic and hedonistic purposes.
- Animals used in entertainment suffer greatly.
- Laws that supposedly protect animals used for entertainment are weak and rarely enforced.

Animals Should Be Used for Entertainment

"While people can learn much about animals from books, movies, and the Internet, there is nothing that will open human eyes, minds, and hearts to these wonderful creatures more quickly and thoroughly than seeing an animal in the flesh and observing its behavior in a habitat display or with a trainer or handler."

—The National Animal Interest Alliance, an organization that promotes balancing the humane treatment of animals with entrenched cultural practices.

National Animal Interest Alliance, "Animals in Entertainment." www.naiaonline.org.

Consider these questions as you read:

1. Do you think that cultural traditions justify using animals for entertainment? Why or why not?
2. Consider a hunter's argument that his or her hobby helps feed people and culls overpopulated wildlife species. Do you think these factors legitimize this form of entertainment? Why or why not?
3. Think back to a time when you visited a zoo, aquarium, or wild animal park. Did your visit provide you with a good educational experience? Why or why not? If you have never visited such a facility, what do you think you might get out of it?

Editor's note: The discussion that follows presents common arguments made in support of this perspective, reinforced by facts, quotes, and examples from various sources.

Using animals for entertainment is an important part of human culture. Laws protect these animals from abuse and neglect, and entertainment venues like zoos have numerous educational and ecological benefits. Engaging with animals in these settings is perfectly moral and helps people stay connected to the natural world.

An Integral Part of Human Culture

Visiting zoos, aquariums, and circuses is a wholesome, traditional family activity. For generations, circuses and animal parks like SeaWorld have provided families and communities with a positive experience and a way to appreciate the intelligence of animals and what they are capable of if they have the right training. In fact, circus spokespersons report that many people express disappointment when told that some circuses have terminated their elephant acts. "People call and ask, 'Will you have the elephants?,'" states Jim Berg, the spokesman for a Minnesota Shriners club that raises charitable funds through the Osman Shrine Circus. "The animals are what make it the true American circus."[46] Millions of people agree: according to the Association of Zoos and Aquariums (AZA), over 181 million people visit accredited zoos and aquariums in America each year, more than the combined number who attend professional sports events annually.

> "People call and ask, 'Will you have the elephants?' The animals are what make it the true American circus."[46]
>
> —Jim Berg, the spokesman for a Minnesota Shriners club that raises charitable funds through the Osman Shrine Circus

The use of animals in movies and television is another time-honored tradition. Documentaries have revealed that animal actors are trained using positive reinforcement methods, and many love their work. Some, like German shepherd Rin Tin Tin, even receive best-actor votes from the public. In fact, Rin Tin Tin was so popular in the twenty-six movies in which he starred in the 1930s that the revenues he brought in helped prevent the Warner Brothers movie studio from filing for bankruptcy. Other actors, like Keiko the killer whale, who starred in the *Free Willy* movies in the 1990s and early twenty-first century, became beloved celebrities as well.

Activities like hunting and fishing are also beloved pastimes that are critical to culture in certain places. The US Fish and Wildlife Service reports that in 2015 nearly 36 million hunters purchased hunting licenses nationwide. When asked why they hunt, many people speak of cultural aspects, such as camaraderie and family. "I hunt to keep the tradition going," states New Hampshire hunter Jonathan Partridge. "Hopefully, I will be able to hand down the traditions and knowledge you can only learn in the woods."[47] Other hunters point out that hunting allows them to stock their freezers with high-quality meat. Wayne Caflin, for instance, states that he hunts because the meat "is healthier than meat purchased in the store."[48]

Laws Protect Animals That Are Used for Entertainment

Still, some animal rights activists have raised legitimate points about instances of animal cruelty, and this is why organizations like the American Humane Association (AHA) focus on ensuring that these traditions and pastimes are governed by proper regulations that enforce humane practices. As the AHA website explains, animals that perform in circuses or other venues "are an ongoing part of our society and culture. . . . As such, we support improvements in animal welfare legislation . . . [and] a high standard of care."[49] The AHA thus sponsors programs such as the Film and Television Unit, which ensures that animals used in movies and on television sets are treated safely and humanely at all times, with access to fresh water, food, exercise, and rest. It also requires that these animals be retired to humane sanctuaries when their performing days are over.

Zoos, circuses, and other venues that exhibit animals are subject to laws and regulations that protect the animals. For example, the AWA requires circuses and zoos—and the trainers and veterinarians who interact with animals—to be licensed and periodically inspected by USDA agents. This law also specifies that animals must be protected from things like "trauma, overheating, excessive cooling, behavioral stress, physical harm and unnecessary discomfort."[50]

Hunters and fur trappers are also bound by laws that require licensing and forbid torture and the killing of endangered species. For instance, the 2016–2017 Hunting and Trapping Guide for the Canadian province of Newfoundland and Labrador states, "Humane trapping is every trapper's

Zoos and Aquariums Educate Even as They Entertain

Entertainment is a great way to reach people—and zoos and aquariums excel at both entertainment and education, which is all the justification one needs for exhibiting animals in entertainment settings. The Association of Zoos & Aquariums (AZA), which accredits 232 zoos and aquariums in nine countries, emphasizes that these institutions provide meaningful educational experiences for students and families, helping participants learn about animals and animal conservation as well as connecting people to nature. A 2015 AZA study provided statistics on how many people participated in these educational programs and how many institutions offered such programs.

- **STEM programming reached 2.3 million participants.**

- **51 million elementary, middle, and high school students participated in education programs.**

- **More than 77 million people were reached through education programs that connect people to nature.**

- **100 institutions reported offering programs that encouraged participants to spend more time in nature.**

- **36 percent of reporting institutions provided teacher training.**

- **84 percent of institutions provided programs that focus on connecting people to nature.**

Source: Association of Zoos & Aquariums, "2015 Annual Report on Conservation and Science." www.aza.org.

responsibility. It ensures that the taking of furbearers is conducted with the least amount of stress to the target animals."[51] Among the cruelties that these and similar regulations prohibit is the use of tooth-edged traps, which cause animals severe and unnecessary pain. Hunters and trappers are also subject to laws that restrict the number of animals they may kill and the seasons and areas in which hunting may occur. This helps ensure the stability and sustainability of animal populations. "Hunting and trapping . . . seasons are set to coincide with animal life cycles," explains the Illinois Department of Natural Resources. "Trapping is not allowed when furbearers are giving birth to and raising their young."[52]

Ecological Benefits

Some activities in which animals are used for entertainment have significant ecological benefit. For instance, trappers and hunters help cull overpopulated species, which helps preserve vital ecosystems. A 2014 report on deer hunting by scientists with the British Deer Society and the Game and Wildlife Conservation Trust explains how hunters play a critical role in wildlife management in Great Britain: "Because major mammalian predators were eliminated from the UK long ago, human management of wild deer populations is essential. . . . Culling using a high-powered rifle is generally accepted as the most humane method of controlling wild deer numbers."[53] All over the world hunters help cull overpopulated species, from crows in Utah to wolves in Norway to swans and geese in New York.

Zoos and aquariums also benefit the environment by breeding endangered or nearly extinct species in captivity and reintroducing them into their native habitats when possible. One example of how captive-breeding programs have benefited conservation efforts is the Arabian oryx, which was hunted to extinction in the wild by 1972. The Phoenix Zoo started a captive-breeding and reintroduction program, and by 2016 about a thousand Arabian oryx were once again living in their native habitats in the Middle East. Other examples of the many species that zoos have saved from extinction are the red wolf, the California condor, and the European bison.

Zoos and aquariums help protect endangered (and nonendangered) animals in other ways as well. Animals who live at zoos and aquariums are protected from starvation, poachers (people who illegally hunt and kill animals), and animals that would otherwise eat them. They also receive regular veterinary care, which helps them stay healthy and live longer lives. "Animals in zoos and aquariums today can live longer, healthier, and richer lives than their forbearers ever did in the wild,"[54] says AHA president and chief executive officer Robin Ganzert.

Educational Experiences

Finally, entertainment venues like zoos and animal parks provide valuable educational experiences for people of all ages. Surveys by the AZA indicate that visiting a zoo or aquarium helps the public understand and value wildlife and motivates many people—young and old—to help conserve the natural world. "Visitors believe zoos and aquariums play an important role in conservation education," explains the AZA website. "When they experience a stronger connection to nature, [they] are prompted to reconsider their role in environmental problems and conservation action and see themselves as part of the solution as a result of their visit."[55]

> "Animals in zoos and aquariums today can live longer, healthier, and richer lives than their forbearers ever did in the wild."[54]
>
> —American Humane Association president Robin Ganzert

A 2012 study of visitors at the Edinburgh Zoo by psychologists at the Scottish Primate Research Group supports the educational value of these facilities. Researchers discovered that the zoo's investment in exhibits in which biologists explained their field research led visitors to spend significantly more time at each exhibit. In addition, "parents were often seen explaining the research to their children," which led the study authors to conclude that well-planned exhibits lead visitors "to invest time in learning more and passing on this knowledge."[56] In this way, zoos—and other entertainment venues that feature animals—help ensure that future generations will value animals and support positive ways to include them in their lives.

Animals Should Not Be Used for Entertainment

"Zoos teach people that it is acceptable to interfere with animals and keep them locked up in captivity, where they are bored, cramped, lonely, deprived of all control over their lives, and far from their natural homes."

—People for the Ethical Treatment of Animals, an animal rights organization

People for the Ethical Treatment of Animals, "Zoos: Pitiful Prisons." www.peta.org.

Consider these questions as you read:

1. Does knowing about the harsh training methods and confinement that large circus animals experience affect your willingness to support and enjoy circuses? Why or why not?
2. Do you think zoo officials were justified in killing Marius the giraffe because he was no longer valuable to the Copenhagen Zoo? Explain your answer.
3. What is your opinion about how hunting and fishing are commonly referred to as "sport"? Should these pastimes be considered forms of entertainment? Why or why not?

Editor's note: The discussion that follows presents common arguments made in support of this perspective, reinforced by facts, quotes, and examples taken from various sources.

Using animals for entertainment is wrong because animals do not exist for human pleasure or economic gain. Wild animals suffer greatly in captivity, and laws designed to protect them from abuse are weak and rarely enforced. For these reasons and more, it is immoral to use animals in these ways.

Most Americans Are Concerned About Entertainment Animals

A 2015 Gallup poll indicated that most Americans are somewhat or very concerned about the treatment of animals in circuses, marine parks, and other entertainment settings. Although Gallup did not specify which factors led to respondents' concerns, analysts believe that publicity and documentaries such as *Blackfish*, a 2013 movie about how orcas are treated in captivity, influenced these perceptions.

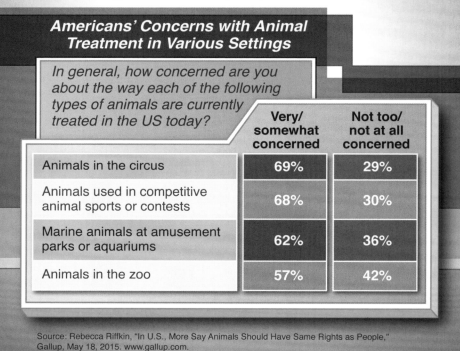

Americans' Concerns with Animal Treatment in Various Settings

In general, how concerned are you about the way each of the following types of animals are currently treated in the US today?	Very/ somewhat concerned	Not too/ not at all concerned
Animals in the circus	69%	29%
Animals used in competitive animal sports or contests	68%	30%
Marine animals at amusement parks or aquariums	62%	36%
Animals in the zoo	57%	42%

Source: Rebecca Riffkin, "In U.S., More Say Animals Should Have Same Rights as People," Gallup, May 18, 2015. www.gallup.com.

Economics Drive Decisions, Not Animal Welfare

Animals should not be used for entertainment; such endeavors exploit animals for selfish human desires and for economic gain, with little or no regard for the comfort or needs of the animals. Indeed, undercover investigators routinely find that animals in entertainment venues tend to live in cramped quarters and endure mistreatment and neglect.

For example, although the Ringling Bros. circus discontinued its elephant acts, most other circus companies still feature these acts because they are so popular with the public. Yet undercover investigations by PETA and the HSUS, along with testimony by veterinarians and former circus workers, reveal that the elephants suffer profoundly, routinely enduring three-day train rides with no breaks. As many as five elephants are crammed into each boxcar, standing in gallons of their own feces. Veterinarians find that most circus elephants have tuberculosis, herpes, and infected bullhook wounds. Most are lame from ulcerated feet and twisted legs that result from being tied up and forced to perform unnatural tricks. Thus, even after they are retired from circus life, these elephants will always have twisted legs and other problems from years of abuse. Although circuses may be fun for people, they are miserable for animals.

Zoos also make decisions based on economics and human whims rather than on animal welfare. For example, in 2014 zookeepers at the Copenhagen Zoo shot Marius, an eighteen-month-old giraffe, and fed him to zoo lions after determining that his inferior genes made him unsuitable for breeding. This happened despite widespread protests and offers from several zoos to adopt Marius, who was healthy. The Copenhagen Zoo's scientific director, Bengt Holst, explained that Marius was a so-called surplus giraffe because his genes were not economically valuable. Zoos, particularly in Europe, kill thousands of surplus animals each year. In some cases, animals are labeled surplus when they are no longer cute babies that admission-paying zoo visitors fawn over, and they are killed to make room for baby animals. Holst says, "We don't do it to be cruel; we do it to ensure a healthy population."[57] However, it is hard to describe the killing of a young, healthy living creature as anything else.

Hunting Is Murder

In many ways, hunting and similar so-called sports are even worse than circuses and zoos because hunters make sport out of murdering innocent animals. However, since hunting has long been considered to be a gentlemanly activity, wealthy hunters pay to keep even the most abusive subsports like trophy hunting legal. Trophy-hunting tours in Africa range from a few thousand to hundreds of thousands of dollars, depending on the animals hunted and the cost of local fees and accommodations. For example, in 2015 Texas trophy hunter Corey Knowlton paid $350,000 to hunt an endangered black rhinoceros in Namibia.

Animal advocates have long objected to hunters deriving entertainment from murder. In 1894, for example, British animal rights pioneer Henry S. Salt called killing animals for fun "the most wanton and indefensible of all possible violations of the principle of animals' rights. . . . To seek one's own amusement out of the death-pangs of other beings, this is saddening stupidity indeed."[58] In modern times, many people agree with this assessment; a 2015 Marist poll found 56 percent of Americans oppose hunting for sport.

> "To seek one's own amusement out of the death-pangs of other beings, this is saddening stupidity indeed."[58]
>
> —British animal rights pioneer and author Henry S. Salt

Although hunters enjoy themselves, their victims and the victims' families suffer greatly. "This unnecessary, violent form of 'entertainment' rips animal families apart and leaves countless animals orphaned or badly injured when hunters miss their targets,"[59] PETA notes. In fact, studies indicate that up to 50 percent of animals shot with crossbows do not die after the first shot. Cecil, a black-maned lion killed by Minnesota trophy hunter Walter Palmer in 2015 in Zimbabwe, suffered for forty hours after he was shot with a crossbow. Palmer finally killed Cecil with a rifle.

Cecil's death "sparked what's been called the biggest global response to a wildlife story ever,"[60] according to *National Geographic*. Palmer received so many threats that he went into hiding for weeks. Several nations and airlines tightened restrictions on trophy hunting and on shipping trophy-hunted animals in response to the outrage. However, trophy hunters still pay thousands of dollars to sneak their trophies past inspectors.

Captivity Is Wrong

Captivity, too, is detrimental to wild animals. The USDA and animal rights organizations have confirmed that animals like tigers suffer most in the tiny cages in which they are confined at unaccredited roadside and petting zoos. However, animal advocates note that accommodations at reputable zoos and animal parks are also unhealthy. "Animals are often prevented from doing most of the things that are natural and important to them, like running, roaming, flying, climbing, foraging, choosing a partner, and being with others of their own kind,"[61] PETA explains. For instance, many zoo elephants are forcibly taken from their mothers soon after birth, whereas wild mothers suckle their babies for two to four years and socialize them until they are teenagers. Studies indicate that these separations are emotionally devastating for babies and mothers and lead to fearful and sometimes aggressive behavior.

Simply being in captivity is stressful, and many zoo and aquarium animals display stress-linked behaviors like pacing, rocking back and forth, and damaging their own bodies. Veterinarians call captivity-related stress and the subsequent behaviors *zoochoses*. One example is when captive orcas swim in endless circles or float listlessly in their small tanks. In contrast, wild orcas swim as much as 100 miles (161 km) per day and live in large social groups.

Experts believe stress also triggers aggressive behavior in many orcas at Sea-World and other amusement parks. Numerous orcas have attacked their trainers. Tilikum, a 12,500 pound (5,670 kg) SeaWorld orca, killed two trainers—Keltie Byrne in 1991 and Dawn Brancheau in 2010. "Killer whales don't attack humans in the wild," says former orca trainer Jeff Ventre. "What we've seen in these injuries to people is a direct byproduct of the stress associated with captivity."[62]

> "Killer whales don't attack humans in the wild. What we've seen in these injuries to people is a direct byproduct of the stress associated with captivity."[62]
>
> —Former orca trainer Jeff Ventre

Stress and other factors related to captivity also contribute to earlier-than-normal natural deaths and to unnatural deaths. For instance, British biologist Ros Clubb found that the average life span for African elephants in zoos is 16.9 years, compared to 56 years in the wild. Marius's death is one example of an early, unnatural death; another is Harambe, the western lowland gorilla shot by Cincinnati Zoo officials on May 28, 2016, after a three-year-old boy jumped into Harambe's enclosure.

Harambe showed no aggression; indeed, primate biologist Jane Goodall later stated that photos showed Harambe protectively putting his arm around the boy. However, zoo decision makers decided Harambe was a threat. "Captivity is the real crime here," notes PETA. "Yet again, captivity has taken an animal's life."[63]

Animal Entertainment Is Not Educational

Furthermore, claims about the educational value of places like zoos are exaggerated. Neuroscientist Lori Marino and her colleagues evaluated an AZA study that claimed that people learned a great deal and were motivated to participate in conservation efforts after they visited zoos and aquariums. However, Marino's team determined that the study was poorly designed and that its conclusions were biased since it did not actually measure peoples' attitude changes. The AZA researchers simply asked zoo visitors whether they *thought* their attitudes and behaviors had changed, which is different than whether their attitudes actually did change. Numerous scientific studies have proved that asking this type of loaded question without using objective measurements yields invalid results. Marino's group thus concluded, "There remains no compelling evidence for the claim that zoos and aquariums promote attitude change, education, or interest in conservation in visitors."[64]

The lack of educational value stems primarily from the unnatural environment inherent in captivity. "While a number of zoos make an effort to provide some sort of education, they mostly teach people how animals react in captive situations . . . to boredom, depression, and stress," explains the Last Chance for Animals organization. "Simply showing animals in extremely restrictive spaces misinforms patrons by misrepresenting what those animals' lives naturally consist of."[65] Most animal entertainment opponents advise people who wish to learn about animals to respectfully visit them in their native habitats.

Chapter Four

Is It Ethical to Experiment on Animals?

It Is Ethical to Experiment on Animals

- Medical and scientific progress depends on experiments with animals.
- There are no viable alternatives to using animals in experiments.
- Advancing human medical science is worth any animal suffering involved.
- Laws prevent experimenters from imposing any suffering on animals that is not scientifically warranted.

The Debate at a Glance

It Is Not Ethical to Experiment on Animals

- The suffering and abuse experimental animals endure far outweigh any potential medical breakthroughs.
- Animal experimentation rarely, if ever, leads to new treatments for human diseases.
- There are viable alternatives to animal experimentation, including computer models and in vitro studies.
- Anticruelty laws do not effectively protect animals used in research.

It Is Ethical to Experiment on Animals

"If we want to advance our biological knowledge toward the end of creating new medical treatment and cures, we absolutely must allow animal research."

—Attorney and author Wesley J. Smith

Wesley J. Smith, "Animal Rights War on Medical Cures," *National Review*, May 17, 2014. www.national review.com.

Consider these questions as you read:

1. Do you agree with claims by researchers that advancing human health is worth exposing laboratory animals to suffering and death? Why or why not?
2. Some people have called psychologist Edward Taub an animal torturer, but others regard him as a dedicated scientist who brought hope to thousands of paralyzed people. In your opinion, which label is appropriate, and why?
3. What is your opinion about the US government's 2015 ban on experiments that involve chimpanzees? Do you think the ban will significantly impact human health? Why or why not?

Editor's note: The discussion that follows presents common arguments made in support of this perspective, reinforced by facts, quotes, and examples from various sources.

It is ethical to experiment on animals, even when this involves pain and death. This is because the potential benefits to human health far outweigh any concerns about animal welfare. Since human health and well-being are the most important aspects of human existence, using animals to save human lives is widely accepted and morally just. As philosophy professor Carl Cohen puts it, "If the common killing of them for food or convenience is right, the less common but more humane uses of animals in the service of medical science are certainly not less right."[66]

Medical Progress Depends on Animal Experimentation

Medical progress depends on animal experimentation. "For more than a hundred years, virtually every medical breakthrough in human and animal health has been the direct result of research using animals,"[67] states the California Biomedical Research Association. Examples include studies on guinea pigs and nonhuman primates in the 1990s that led to the first new asthma treatment in twenty years (drugs called leukotriene-receptor agonists), and studies on chimpanzees in the 1950s that led to the first polio vaccine. Before the vaccine was developed, polio killed millions and disabled millions more each year. Vaccines that prevent rabies, distemper, and feline leukemia in animals were also born from animal research.

One of the most controversial breakthroughs resulted from psychologist Edward Taub's research at the Institute for Behavioral Research in Silver Spring, Maryland. Taub's studies on macaque monkeys proved that neuroplasticity—the brain's ability to rewire itself after its normal connections are severed—can be induced by forcing animals to move paralyzed limbs. After an undercover animal rights activist convinced authorities to charge Taub with animal cruelty in 1981, he spent several years legally clearing his name. He finally resumed his work at the University of Alabama, Birmingham, where he established constraint-induced movement therapy as a way to help stroke victims recover the use of disabled limbs. "Today stroke victims have hope because Taub resumed his work at the University of Alabama,"[68] writes NAIA president Patti Strand.

> "If the common killing of them for food or convenience is right, the less common but more humane uses of animals in the service of medical science are certainly not less right."[66]
>
> —University of Michigan philosophy professor Carl Cohen

Had Taub not continued his experiments on animals, people like James Faust would be permanently disabled. The right side of Faust's body was paralyzed by a stroke, but after several weeks of therapy at Taub's clinic, he regained the use of his right arm and leg. "The doctors weren't sure I would make it through the night when I had my stroke," he says. "Now I manage to mow my grass—and I've got almost two acres."[69]

No Viable Alternatives

In addition, there are no viable alternatives to animal research; without it, medical progress would stagnate and scientists would have to endanger human lives to investigate experimental treatments. The need for animal testing stems from the fact that the complex interactions between body systems in living creatures make it "impossible to explore, explain, or predict the course of diseases or the effects of possible treatments without observing and testing the entire living system of an animal,"[70] explains the California Biomedical Research Association. Thus, it is not always possible to use alternative methods like computer models (known as in silico studies) or human cells outside a living body (in vitro studies) to predict the effects of a new disease treatment.

> "For more than a hundred years, virtually every medical breakthrough in human and animal health has been the direct result of research using animals."[67]
>
> —The California Biomedical Research Association

The fact that animals and humans share much DNA and physiology also makes animals important for medical research. For instance, mouse and human DNA are more than 98 percent identical, and chimpanzee and human DNA are 99 percent identical. These animals' systems are therefore similar enough to those of humans to make accurate predictions about responses to disease treatments. In some cases, chimpanzees are the only animals that develop certain human diseases. Albert Sabin, who developed the first polio vaccine, stressed that his research depended on chimpanzees because they are the only animals that acquire and react to the polio virus like humans do.

This is why the 2015 National Institutes of Health (NIH) announcement that chimpanzees can no longer be used in biomedical and behavioral research in the United States was so devastating to medical science. The NIH did this because chimpanzees are now endangered, but in doing so it set off a firestorm of criticism from researchers who believe chimp studies are essential for medical progress. The Federation of American Societies for Experimental Biology, for instance, stated that research on diseases like viral hepatitis would languish since chimps are the only nonhuman animals susceptible to infection with the five main hepatitis viruses. Indeed, chimp research led to diagnostic tests and vaccines for the hepatitis A and B viruses in the 1990s and 1980s, respectively, cutting human infection rates for hepatitis A by 92 percent and hepatitis B by 82 percent. There is still no vaccine for hepatitis C, which affects 2.7 to 3.9 million Americans, according to the Centers for Disease Control and Prevention.

Researchers Cannot Impose Unjustified Suffering

Laws like the AWA require that scientists treat laboratory animals humanely. They also require scientists to demonstrate that any pain the animals suffer is scientifically necessary. These regulations make sure animal experimentation is undertaken morally and ethically. In addition, research institutions have Institutional Animal Care and Use Committees (IACUCs) made up of experimenters, animal care technicians, and veterinarians who review each experiment proposal. The IACUCs have the authority to reject proposals that committee members believe involve undue suffering for animals.

The NIH also oversees biomedical research. It requires scientists to follow rules about humane practices published in its *Guide for the Care and Use of Laboratory Animals*. In addition, a private organization called the American Association for the Accreditation of Laboratory Animal Care inspects research facilities and can deny accreditation if evidence of inhumane care is found.

Researchers are also bound by moral principles known as the Three Rs, which were introduced by scientists William Russell and Rex Burch in 1959. The Three Rs prescribe the replacement, reduction, and refinement

The Majority of People Support Using Animals in Biomedical Research

A 2016 North American study by researchers at the University of Alberta in Canada reveals that most members of the public and even greater numbers of medical students believe it is ethical to use animals in biomedical research. Support for animal research is greater among medical students than among the general public, but one of the primary reasons people in both groups support such research is that it benefits humans.

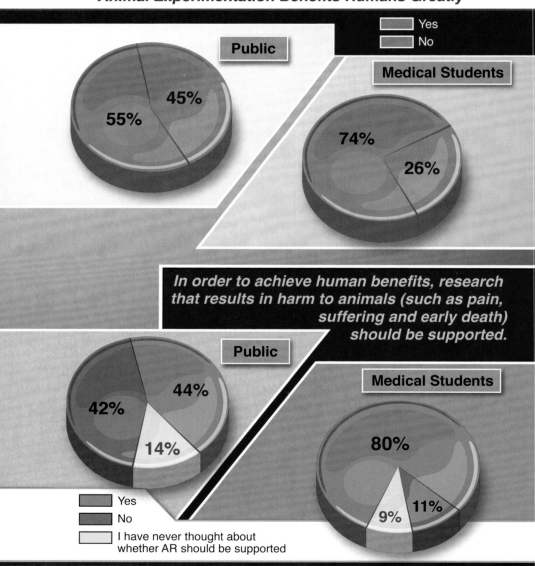

Animal Experimentation Benefits Humans Greatly

Yes
No

Public
45%
55%

Medical Students
74%
26%

In order to achieve human benefits, research that results in harm to animals (such as pain, suffering and early death) should be supported.

Public
44%
42%
14%

Medical Students
80%
9%
11%

Yes
No
I have never thought about whether AR should be supported

Source: Ari R. Joffe et al., "The Ethics of Animal Research: A Survey of the Public and Scientists in North America," *BMC Medical Ethics*, March 2016. https://bmcmedethics.biomedcentral.com.

of studies that harm animals. Scientists must demonstrate that using animals is the best, or only, option, and that cell cultures, computer models, or other methods are not applicable to a particular project. The Three Rs also limit an experiment's intended uses. "The use of animals in science is acceptable ONLY if it promises to contribute to understanding of fundamental biological principles, or to the development of knowledge that can reasonably be expected to benefit humans, animals or the environment,"[71] explains the Canadian Council on Animal Care.

Animals Are Important in Science Education

The Three Rs apply not only to biomedical research but also to science education, especially that that features classroom animal dissection. Although dissection is controversial, it too is guided by reasonable principles and ethics. Many schools, for example, allow students to opt out of dissections and to use alternatives like computer models. But most science teachers and organizations like the National Science Teachers Association (NSTA) favor traditional dissection because they believe students learn best when they use real animals. "There isn't any substitute for the real thing," says David Evans of the NSTA. "You can study the physics of music and study the great composers, but that's not going to make you a violinist. Learning is a sensory experience and touching things matters."[72] Canadian teachers who participated in a 2012 study on classroom dissection also noted that dissection prepares students for scientific or medical careers and teaches them to respect living creatures while advancing science. For all of these reasons, using animals in classroom teaching and research is ethical because scientific and medical progress depends on the next generation to continue advancing these important endeavors.

It Is Not Ethical to Experiment on Animals

"Imagine spending your entire life as a hospital patient or prisoner, and this will only begin to approximate the life of an animal in a laboratory. What happens to you can range from uncomfortable to agonizing to deadly—and you are helpless to defend yourself."

—The New England Anti-Vivisection Society

New England Anti-Vivisection Society, "Animals in Research." www.neavs.org.

Consider these questions as you read:

1. Do you think dissecting animals in biology classes sends students the message that animal lives are not valuable? Explain your answer.
2. Do you think exposing millions of animals to painful experiments and death each year is worth it if even one experiment saves human lives? Why or why not?
3. Scientists claim that they never subject laboratory animals to unnecessary suffering, but videos from numerous animal rights activists show animals enduring what most people would consider torture. What is your opinion about how torture should be defined? Should the definition rely on assessments made by experimenters, laypersons, or bioethicists? Explain your answer.

Editor's note: The discussion that follows presents common arguments made in support of this perspective, reinforced by facts, quotes, and examples taken from various sources.

Animal experimentation is unethical for several reasons. For one, the suffering and abuse animals endure during experiments far outweigh any potential medical breakthroughs. In addition, animal experimentation rarely, if ever, leads to new treatments for human diseases. There are many viable alternatives to animal experimentation, including computer models and in vitro studies. For these reasons and more, it is wrong to inflict suffering, disease, and death on millions of sentient creatures in the name of medical science.

The Suffering Is Vast

Laboratory animals suffer immensely. They are confined to tiny cages, forced to undergo unnecessary operations, exposed to nasty germs and cancers, and submitted to other torture. "If anyone other than white-coated scientists treated monkeys, dogs, cats, rabbits, pigs, and so forth as they do behind the locked doors of the animal lab, he or she would be prosecuted for cruelty,"[73] states primate biologist Jane Goodall.

In one dramatic illustration of cruelty, Alex Pacheco, a cofounder of PETA, worked undercover in Edward Taub's laboratory at the Institute for Behavioral Research. He took videos that documented how Taub's macaque monkeys lived in tiny, feces-coated cages and were fed rarely, forcibly restrained, and given painful electric shocks until they moved their disabled limbs. Worse, Taub disabled these animals' limbs by cutting the nerves that controlled them. Yet after Taub was cleared of animal cruelty charges based on a legal technicality, he was allowed to resume his torture of animals because he told regulators that any discomfort was scientifically necessary.

> "If anyone other than white-coated scientists treated monkeys, dogs, cats, rabbits, pigs, and so forth as they do behind the locked doors of the animal lab, he or she would be prosecuted for cruelty."[73]
>
> —Primate biologist Jane Goodall

Animal Research Rarely Applies to Humans

In addition to the vast suffering it causes, much animal research is done in vain. In fact, animal research rarely benefits human health because of the significant differences in human and animal physiology. For example, many drugs that benefit animals are dangerous to humans and vice versa. In 2004 the arthritis drug Vioxx was taken off the market after it caused fatal heart attacks in about thirty-eight thousand people. Animal testing previously indicated Vioxx was safe. Another drug, aspirin, is safe for pregnant women but causes severe birth defects in mice, rats, dogs, cats, rabbits, and monkeys. John J. Pippin and Kristie Sullivan of the Physicians Committee for Responsible Medicine (PCRM) state that up to 50 percent of the drugs approved by the US Food and Drug Administration are withdrawn from the market or are relabeled because of unforeseen problems. They warn that doctors who rely on animal tests to predict drug safety in humans "are willing to risk the health of patients."[74]

Other types of animal research are also not applicable to human health. For instance, numerous studies use monkeys to find a vaccine for HIV, which causes AIDS in humans. However, the virus that sickens monkeys is different from the one that affects people. As geneticist Jarrod Baily explains, scientists have spent billions testing dozens of AIDS vaccines, and "almost all of these vaccines protected chimpanzees from HIV infection, but none worked in humans."[75]

Researchers Rarely Try Alternatives

The ethical wrong of vivisection is compounded by the fact that scientists rarely use viable alternatives like human volunteers. They also do not take good advantage of in vitro studies (which use a test tube or petri dish or take place outside a living thing) or in silico studies (which feature computer modeling or simulation). Indeed, many products can successfully be tested without experimenting on animals. Consider the alternative testing methods known as EpiOcular and EpiDerm. These are in vitro cell cultures derived from human eye cells and skin cells, respectively, that have been used to test cosmetics and other products. Before these in vitro tests were invented, scientists tested products for toxicity by spraying them into rabbits' eyes or applying huge doses to their skin. In addition to being more humane, in vitro tools have been found to be more accurate than animal testing. The MatTek Corporation, which produces EpiDerm, proved that it correctly identified skin irritants 100 percent of the

Opposition to Use of Animals in Scientific Research Is Growing

A Gallup poll published in 2015 found that opposition to the use of animals in scientific research is growing. In a 2009 poll, 43 percent of US adults opposed the use of animals in scientific research. When asked the same question in a 2014 poll, 50 percent said they opposed the use of animals for this purpose.

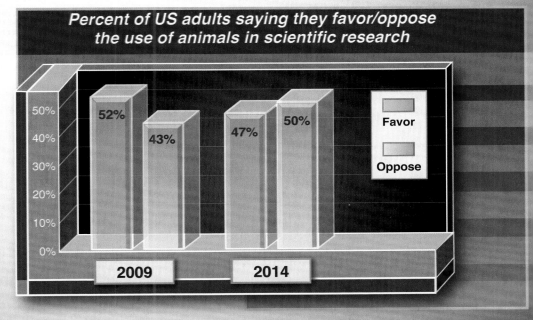

Percent of US adults saying they favor/oppose the use of animals in scientific research

Source: Cary Funk and Lee Rainie, "Opinion About the Use of Animals in Research," Pew Research Center, July 1, 2015. www.pewinternet.org.

time, compared to 60 percent accuracy for tests on the skin of live rabbits.

Scientists at Harvard University's Wyss Institute have developed another type of product that combines in vitro and in silico technologies. Known as organs-on-chips, these are computer microchips lined with human cells that can mimic the composition and function of specific human organs, such as lungs, kidneys, or skin. These are proving to be ideal for identifying new cellular targets for drugs to treat certain diseases and for testing new compounds on functioning organs or combinations of organs. Although researchers are required to consider alternative methods for each experiment, investigations reveal that few researchers actually give the alternatives serious consideration. This is why animal welfare agencies estimate that approximately 115 million laboratory animals are still experimented on worldwide each year.

Physician C. Ray Greek and his wife, veterinarian Jean Swingle Greek, believe that economic motives underlie much of the resistance to alternative methods. "Alternative protocols are not peddled by huge corporations, which have both the money and incentive to sway public sentiment,"[76] the Greeks write in their book *Sacred Cows and Golden Geese*. They note that animal research is a huge industry, and companies that breed, ship, sell, and use laboratory animals would lose money if less animal research took place.

Animal Research Breeds Insensitivity

Animal experimentation is also unethical because it teaches that abusing animals is acceptable. Australian veterinarian Andrew Knight notes that veterinary students who perform animal research become desensitized to animal suffering and later fail to prescribe adequate pain medication to their patients. Studies support these observations. For instance, psychologists at the University of Edinburgh found that first-year veterinary students showed greater awareness of animal fear, pain, and boredom than fourth-year students, who had learned to emotionally detach themselves.

Similar concerns about medical students led American medical schools to phase out the use of live animals as teaching tools. As of June 2016, students at all accredited medical schools learned to insert breathing tubes and other such techniques on human cadavers rather than animals. Most high school and college biology curriculums, however, still include animal dissections. Dissections, states Goodall, teach students "that it is ethically acceptable to perpetrate, in the name of science, what from the point of view of the animals, would certainly qualify as torture."[77]

Laws Do Not Protect Laboratory Animals

Finally, animal experimentation is not made more ethical by the laws that are supposed to protect such subjects from harm. Even though Congress passed the AWA in 1966 to protect lab animals from undue suffering and harm, this and other laws have not been enforced. Law enforcement agencies routinely fail to punish scientists who subject animals to unnecessary suffering. For example, in 2011 the PCRM filed complaints against Wayne State University cardiovascular researcher Donal O'Leary for forcing a dog named Queenie to run on a treadmill despite postsurgery pain and complications. The PCRM and veterinarians analyzed O'Leary's laboratory records and determined that Queenie and more than sixty other dogs suffered unnecessarily and "produced nothing to advance [human] heart failure prevention or management."[78] The PCRM filed numerous requests for the government and the university to shut the laboratory down, but USDA inspectors stated that any perceived cruelty was scientifically necessary. As of late 2016, the PCRM was still fighting this battle.

> "Any study that will advance science, even in a very small way, can be used to justify tremendous amounts of animal suffering, as long as the suffering is necessary to the advance."[79]
>
> —Yale University bioethicist and attorney Stephen R. Latham

In addition to not being enforced, the AWA does not cover the rats, mice, and birds that are used in 99 percent of all experiments. The research guide put out by the NIH covers all vertebrates, but the internal review boards for research institutions can override this guide and the AWA if they think an experiment's scientific value warrants it. "The result is that any study that will advance science, even in a very small way, can be used to justify tremendous amounts of animal suffering as long as the suffering is necessary to the advance,"[79] explains Yale University bioethicist and attorney Stephen R. Latham. Despite the existence of laws, the reality is that researchers can do practically anything to lab animals if they claim it is scientifically necessary.

Source Notes

Overview: The Animal Rights Debate

1. Quoted in Jessica Schladebeck, "See It: Animal Rights Protesters Crash Amy Schumer's Book Signing to Blast Comedian for Canada Goose Jacket," *New York Daily News*, August 17, 2016. www.nydailynews.com.
2. Quoted in Wayne Ford, "Athens Zoo Closed Temporarily After Vandals Strike, Let Owl Loose," Online Athens, July 23, 2016. http://onlineathens.com.
3. Gary L. Francione and Robert Garner, *The Animal Rights Debate: Abolition or Regulation?* New York: Columbia University Press, 2010, pp. x, 4.
4. Marc Bekoff, *The Animal Manifesto*. Novato, CA: New World Library, 2010, p. 181.
5. Francione and Garner, *The Animal Rights Debate*, p. 104.
6. North American Animal Liberation Press Office, "When Vivisectors Begin to Die," June 28, 2016. https://animalliberationpressoffice.org.
7. Quoted in Joe Mozingo, "A Thin Line on Animal Rights," *Los Angeles Times*, September 5, 2006. http://articles.latimes.com.
8. Edwin A. Locke, "Animal-Rights Terrorists Take Away Our Right to Life and Liberty," *Los Angeles Daily News*, May 1, 2009. www.dailynews.com.
9. Quoted in Tamara Lush, "The Big Top Comes Down: Ringling Bros. Circus Is Closing," ABC News, January 15, 2017. http://abcnews.go.com.
10. Quoted in Andy Smith, "Forget the Elephants: Ringling Bros. Is Retiring the Big Performers in Response to Changing Attitudes," *Providence (RI) Journal*, April 27, 2016. www.providencejournal.com.
11. Jeremy Bentham, *Introduction to the Principles of Morals and Legislation*. Oxford, UK: Clarendon, 1781, p. 310. www.animal-rights-library.com/texts-c/bentham01.htm.
12. Rupert Hughes, "Animal and Vegetable Rights," *Harper's Monthly Magazine*, November 1901, p. 853. https://books.google.com/books?id=2Po3AQAAMAAJ.
13. Quoted in BrainyQuote, "Mahatma Gandhi Quotes." www.brainyquote.com.

Chapter One: Should Animals Have Rights Similar to Humans?

14. Bentham, *Introduction to the Principles of Morals and Legislation*, p. 311.
15. Peter Singer, "Equality for Animals?," Utilitarian Philosophers. www.utilitarian.net.
16. Quoted in Albert Schweitzer Fellowship, "Philosophy." www.schweitzerfellowship.org.

17. Tom Regan, *The Case for Animal Rights*. Berkeley and Los Angeles: University of California Press, 1983, p. 327.

18. Bekoff, *The Animal Manifesto*, p. 89.

19. Steven M. Wise, "Animal Rights, Animal Wrongs," *Foreign Affairs*, April 28, 2015. www.foreignaffairs.com.

20. Alice Walker, preface to *The Dreaded Comparison: Human and Animal Slavery* by Marjorie Spiegel. New York: Mirror, 1996, p. 14.

21. Peter Singer, *Animal Liberation*. New York: HarperCollins, 1975, p. 243.

22. David Shoemaker, "Moral Address, Moral Responsibility, and the Boundaries of the Moral Community," *Ethics*, vol. 118, no. 1, October 2007, pp. 70–71.

23. Timothy Hsiao, "In Defense of Eating Meat," *Journal of Agricultural and Environmental Ethics*, vol. 28, no. 2, April 2015, pp. 284–85.

24. Damon Linker, "No, Animals Don't Have Rights," *Week*, January 17, 2014. http://theweek.com.

25. Quoted in Bible Hub, "Genesis 1:26." http://biblehub.com.

26. Quoted in Peter and Helen Evans, "Animal Protection or Animal Rights? A Conversation with Brian Saint-Paul," CatholiCity, April 24, 2009. www.catholicity.com.

27. Locke, "Animal-Rights Terrorists Take Away Our Right to Life and Liberty."

28. Quoted in Evans, "Animal Protection or Animal Rights?"

29. National Animal Interest Alliance, "NAIA Policy Statement: Pets and the Community." www.naiaonline.org.

30. National Animal Interest Alliance, "The Pet Guardian Movement." www.naiaonline.org.

Chapter Two: Is It Moral to Eat Animals?

31. Quoted in Evans, "Animal Protection or Animal Rights?"

32. Hsiao, "In Defense of Eating Meat," p. 277.

33. Michael Ruhlman, "Why It's Ethical to Eat Meat," May 29, 2012. http://ruhlman.com.

34. Quoted in Patricia McBroom, "Meat-Eating Was Essential for Human Evolution, Says UC Berkeley Anthropologist Specializing in Diet," University of California, Berkeley, June 14, 1999. www.berkeley.edu.

35. Kadya Araki, "Why All Humans Need to Eat Meat for Health," Breaking Muscle. https://breakingmuscle.com.

36. Benjamin Franklin, *The Autobiography of Benjamin Franklin*. 1868. Reprint, Mineola, NY: Dover, 1996, p. 27.

37. Roger Scruton, *A Political Philosophy*. New York: Continuum, 2006, p. 61.

38. Quoted in Jake Swearington, "Farm Confessional: I Work for an Animal Welfare Organization and I Eat Meat," *Modern Farmer*, April 17, 2014. http://modernfarmer.com.

39. Humane Society of the United States, "Force-Fed Animals." www.humanesociety.org.

40. Alicia Prygoski, "Activists Seek Tighter Slaughter Standards for Chickens, Turkeys," Food Safety News, August 27, 2016. www.foodsafetynews.com.

41. Animal Legal Defense Fund, "Farmed Animals and the Law." www.aldf
.org.

42. Dena Jones, "Poultry Industry Misleads Public About the Humaneness of
Slaughter," *Food Safety News*, April 7, 2015. www.foodsafetynews.com.

43. Government Printing Office, "Title 49—Transportation." www.gpo.gov.

44. National Library of Medicine, "Vegetarian Diet," Medline Plus, December
1, 2014. https://medlineplus.gov.

45. Francione and Garner, *The Animal Rights Debate*, p. 2.

Chapter Three: Should Animals Be Used for Entertainment?

46. Quoted in Sharyn Jackson, "Despite Pressure from Activists, Circus Animal Acts Go On," *Minneapolis Star Tribune*, March 31, 2016. www.star
tribune.com.

47. Quoted in Eric Aldrich, "Why We Hunt," *Wildlife Journal*, September/
October 2015. www.wildlife.state.nh.us.

48. Quoted in Aldrich, "Why We Hunt."

49. American Humane Association, "Animal Welfare Policy and Position Statements." www.americanhumane.org.

50. United States Department of Agriculture, "2.131—Handling of Animals,"
U.S. Government Publishing Office, January 1, 2016. www.gpo.gov.

51. Newfoundland and Labrador Department of Environment and Conservation, "Hunting and Trapping Guide 2016–2017." www.env.gov.nl.ca.

52. Illinois Department of Natural Resources, "Hunting and Trapping Are as
Humane as Possible." www.dnr.state.il.us.

53. Quoted in Nicholas J. Aebischer et al., "Factors Associated with Shooting
Accuracy and Wounding Rate of Four Managed Wild Deer Species in the
UK, Based on Anonymous Field Records from Deer Stalkers," *PLoS One*,
vol. 9, no. 10, October 15, 2014, p. e109698.

54. Robin Ganzert, "Zoos Are Not Prisons. They Improve the Lives of Animals," *Time*, June 13, 2016. http://time.com.

55. Association of Zoos and Aquariums, "Conservation Education." www.aza
.org.

56. Mark T. Bowler et al., "Assessing Public Engagement with Science in a
University Primate Research Centre in a National Zoo," *PLoS One*, vol. 7,
no. 4, April 4, 2012, p. 7.

57. Quoted in Nelson D. Schwartz, "Anger Erupts After Danish Zoo Kills a
'Surplus' Giraffe," *New York Times*, February 9, 2014. www.nytimes.com.

58. Henry S. Salt, *Animals' Rights: Considered in Relation to Social Progress*. New York: MacMillan, 1894, pp. 53–54. https://books.google.com
/books?id=L-zgCGEK01cC.

59. People for the Ethical Treatment of Animals, "Hunting." www.peta.org.

60. Jani Actman, "Cecil the Lion Died One Year Ago—Here's What's Happened Since," *National Geographic*, June 30, 2016. http://news.national
geographic.com.

61. People for the Ethical Treatment of Animals, "Zoos: Pitiful Prisons." www.peta.org.
62. Quoted in Brandon Kim, "Former Trainer Says Killer Whale Captivity Causes Attacks," *Wired*, September 20, 2011. www.wired.com.
63. Angela Henderson, "Pinky, Harambe, Marius, and More: These Horror Stories Show That Zoos Teach People That Wild Animals Are Expendable," *PETA Blog*, August 4, 2016. www.peta.org.
64. Lori Marino et al., "Do Zoos and Aquariums Promote Attitude Change in Visitors? A Critical Evaluation of the American Zoo and Aquarium Study," *Society and Animals*, vol. 18, no. 2, 2010, p. 127.
65. Last Chance for Animals, "Zoos." www.lcanimal.org.

Chapter Four: Is It Ethical to Experiment on Animals?

66. Carl Cohen, "The Case for the Use of Animals in Biomedical Research," *New England Journal of Medicine*, vol. 315, October 2, 1986, p. 869.
67. California Biomedical Research Association, "Why Are Animals Necessary in Biomedical Research?" www.ca-biomed.org.
68. Patti Strand, "Research Pays Off," National Animal Interest Alliance, January 12, 2012. www.naiaonline.org.
69. Quoted in Emily Yellin, "Stroke Survivors Celebrate Success of Restraint Therapy," *New York Times*, June 13, 2000. www.newyorktimes.com.
70. California Biomedical Research Association, "Why Are Animals Necessary in Biomedical Research?"
71. Quoted in Jan Oakley, "Science Teachers and the Dissection Debate: Perspectives on Animal Dissection and Alternatives," *International Journal of Environmental & Science Education*, vol. 7, no. 2, April 2012, p. 263.
72. Quoted in Nicole Shine, "The Battle over High School Animal Dissection," *Pacific Standard*, October 15, 2014. https://psmag.com.
73. Quoted in C. Ray Greek and Jean Swingle Greek, *Sacred Cows and Golden Geese*. New York: Continuum, 2002, p. 9.
74. John J. Pippin and Kristie Sullivan, "Dangerous Medicine: Examples of Animal-Based 'Safety' Tests Gone Wrong," Physicians Committee for Responsible Medicine. www.pcrm.org.
75. Quoted in New England Anti-Vivisection Society, "Research Attributes Lack of HIV/AIDS Vaccine to Use of Chimpanzees," October 6, 2008. www.neavs.org.
76. Greek and Greek, *Sacred Cows and Golden Geese*, p. 100.
77. Jane Goodall, *Through a Window*. Boston: Mariner, 2010, p. 302.
78. Physicians Committee for Responsible Medicine, "Heart Failure Canine Research at Wayne State University: Concerns About Scientific Merit and Cruelty to Animals," February 2014. www.pcrm.org.
79. Stephen R. Latham, *US Law and Animal Experimentation: A Critical Primer*, Hastings Center. http://animalresearch.thehastingscenter.org.

Animal Rights Facts

Using Animals for Entertainment

- Investigators estimate that circus lions and tigers spend more than 95 percent of their time in small cages, and circus horses spend about 98 percent of their time tied up in small areas.
- A study by British biologist Ros Clubb found that captive orcas live an average of nine years, compared to up to one hundred years in the wild.
- Trophy hunter Walter Palmer paid $54,000 for the privilege of killing a lion named Cecil at Zimbabwe's Hwange National Park on July 1, 2015.
- The World Association of Zoos and Aquariums (WAZA) closes zoos that violate its ethics standards.
- A January 2016 Ipsos MORI poll found that only 19 percent of Spaniards ages sixteen to sixty-five support the time-honored tradition of bullfighting, compared to more than 30 percent who supported the sport in 2013. Intense opposition by animal rights groups led numerous towns and the entire Catalonia region of Spain to ban bullfights by late 2016.
- Making a 40-inch (102 cm) fur coat requires killing either sixty mink, forty-two red foxes, forty raccoons, eighteen lynx, or fifteen beavers, according to evolutionary biologist Marc Bekoff.
- WAZA reports that more than 700 million people visit zoos and aquariums around the world each year, and zoos and aquariums contribute about $350 million to animal conservation causes annually.
- There are approximately 750,000 animals in the care of AZA-accredited zoos and aquariums. This includes six thousand different species and one thousand threatened or endangered species.

Using Animals in Research

- The AWA only protects about 1 percent of the animals used in research.
- The USDA reports that approximately eight hundred thousand animals were used in research in the United States in 2015, but this figure

excludes the rodents, birds, and fish that constitute 99 percent of the animals used in research since the AWA does not count them as animals.
- The Johns Hopkins University Center for Alternatives to Animal Testing estimates that about 20 million animals lose their lives to teach students about biology each year.
- Students can learn about animal biology using interactive software like the Digital Frog, DryLab Suite, Sniffy the Virtual Rat, Catlab, and other programs.
- A 2015 Gallup poll found that 67 percent of Americans are concerned about animals used in scientific research.
- In June 2016 the Australian government announced that testing cosmetics on animals will be banned starting in July 2017 in response to polls showing that 85 percent of Australians oppose this practice. Israel, India, and the European Union have already instituted this type of ban.
- The Foundation for Biomedical Research reports that between 1979 and 2015, only one Nobel Prize in Physiology or Medicine was awarded to researchers who did not use animals in their studies.

Using Animals for Food

- According to the UN Food and Agriculture Organization, 347 million tons (315 million metric tons) of meat were produced worldwide in 2014.
- A 2013 study by scientists at the Swedish Institute for Food and Biotechnology found that greenhouse gas emissions from animal food production in Sweden decreased 14 percent between 1990 and 2005 because of reduced production of food animals.
- The US Environmental Protection Agency reports that agriculture, including livestock-associated activities, was responsible for 9 percent of the US greenhouse gas emissions in 2014.
- According to the USDA, each year about 9.5 billion chickens and turkeys, 100 million pigs, and 45 million cattle and sheep are slaughtered for food in the United States.
- A 2015 Harris poll found that 3.4 percent of American adults follow a vegan diet (consuming no animal products) and that around 25

percent are vegetarians who eat no meat but consume milk and egg products.

- A 2013 study conducted by the AHA found that 89 percent of the people surveyed were concerned about the welfare of farm animals, and 74 percent were willing to spend more for meat, eggs, and dairy products from humanely raised animals.
- The Farmers and Hunters Feeding the Hungry Program provided 18 million servings of meat to needy people through food banks between 1997 and 2016; participating hunters donated animals they hunted for this purpose.

Related Organizations and Websites

American Humane Association
1400 Sixteenth St. NW, Suite 360
Washington, DC 20036
website: www.americanhumane.org

The American Humane Association strives to ensure that animals and children are treated compassionately and that their welfare and well-being are addressed by society and government. The organization initiates and promotes programs that protect animals and children from abuse and neglect. It also supports research and education programs that further these goals.

Animal Liberation Front (ALF)
3371 Glendale Blvd., Suite 107
Los Angeles, CA 90039
website: www.animalliberationfront.com

ALF is a loosely organized international organization of independent cells and individuals who advocate using any means necessary, including violence and other illegal methods, to end animal exploitation and suffering.

Center for Consumer Freedom
PO Box 34557
Washington, DC 20043
website: www.consumerfreedom.com

The Center for Consumer Freedom works to counteract the activities of animal rights groups. It believes Americans have the right to make their own choices to eat animals and wear animal products, and to engage in activities of their own choosing.

Federation of American Societies for Experimental Biology (FASEB)
9650 Rockville Pike
Bethesda, MD 20814
website: www.faseb.org

The FASEB is a coalition of scientific societies and biomedical researchers. It shares information about research progress and advocates for the advancement of medical science through research.

The Hastings Center
21 Malcolm Gordon Rd.
Garrison, NY 10524
website: www.thehastingscenter.org

The Hastings Center is a nonpartisan bioethics research institute comprising scholars from the fields of law, philosophy, medicine, education, and other relevant fields who publish books and papers on ethical practices in medicine. One issue the center studies is animal experimentation.

Humane Society of the United States (HSUS)
1255 Twenty-Third St. NW, Suite 450
Washington, DC 20037
website: www.humanesociety.org

The HSUS is the largest animal protection agency in the United States. It provides direct help to animals in many ways, including hands-on care, and offers education programs for the public. It also lobbies lawmakers to pass legislation that protects animals from all types of abuse.

National Animal Interest Alliance (NAIA)
PO Box 66579
Portland, OR 97290
website: www.naiaonline.org

The NAIA is a coalition of business, agricultural, scientific, and recreational groups dedicated to promoting animal welfare and responsible animal use. It seeks to educate the public about issues affecting animals and opposes animal rights extremism.

People for the Ethical Treatment of Animals (PETA)
501 Front St.
Norfolk, VA 23510
website: www.peta.org

PETA is a nonprofit animal rights organization that speaks out and conducts protests and undercover investigations about the inhumane treatment of animals in the food, clothing, entertainment, and research industries. Its website has information about a variety of topics related to animal rights.

Physicians Committee for Responsible Medicine (PCRM)
5100 Wisconsin Ave. NW, Suite 400
Washington, DC 20016
website: www.pcrm.org

The PCRM comprises medical doctors who advocate ending the use of animals in education and research. It also educates the public on issues that involve animal cruelty.

Protect the Harvest
PO Box 10116
Columbia, MO 65205
website: http://protecttheharvest.com

Protect the Harvest is an organization that works to protect the right to hunt, fish, farm, eat meat, and own pets. Its goal is to counteract animal rights groups that seek to deny people the basic rights to live as they see fit.

For Further Research

Books

Noah Berlatsky, *Animal Rights*. Farmington Hills, MI: Greenhaven, 2015.

Susan Hunnicut, *Animal Experimentation*. Farmington Hills, MI: Greenhaven, 2013.

Laura Perdew, *Animal Rights Movement*. North Mankato, MN: ABDO, 2013.

Mark Rowlands, *Animals Rights: All That Matters*. London: Hodder & Stoughton, 2013.

Bonnie Szumski and Jill Karson, *Is Animal Experimentation Ethical?* San Diego: ReferencePoint, 2011.

Patty Taylor, *Animal Rights*. Broomall, PA: Mason Crest, 2016.

Internet Sources

BBC, "Animal Rights." www.bbc.co.uk/ethics/animals/rights/rights_1 .shtml.

Jennifer Latson, "The Sad Story of Laika, the First Dog Launched into Orbit," *Time*, November 3, 2014. http://time.com/3546215/laika-1957.

Damon Linker, "No, Animals Don't Have Rights," *Week*, January 17, 2014. http://theweek.com/articles/452715/no-animals-dont-have-rights.

Speaking of Research, "Medical Benefits." https://speakingofresearch. com/facts/medical-benefits.

Tennille Tracy, "States Target Animal-Rights Activists with Laws Banning Undercover Videos," *Wall Street Journal*, May 29, 2015. www.wsj.com /articles/states-target-animal-rights-activists-with-laws-banning-under cover-videos-1432940473.

Steven M. Wise, "Animals Rights, Animal Wrongs," *Foreign Affairs*, April 28, 2015. www.foreignaffairs.com/articles/2015-04-28/animal -rights-animal-wrongs.

Index

About the Author

Melissa Abramovitz writes fiction and nonfiction for all age groups but specializes in educational nonfiction books and magazine articles for children and teens. She graduated from the University of California, San Diego, with a degree in psychology and is also a graduate of the Institute of Children's Literature.